THE
HUNDRED

DHARMAS

The
Hundred Dharmas

SHASTRA ON THE DOOR TO UNDERSTANDING THE HUNDRED DHARMAS

AN ESSENTIAL TEXT OF THE YOGACARA SCHOOL

The

Hundred Dharmas

BUDDHIST TEXT TRANSLATION SOCIETY

California

Published and translated in North America by:
Buddhist Text Translation Society
4951 Bodhi Way,
Ukiah, CA 95482

Printed in Taiwan on acid-free paper.

Library of Congress Cataloging-in-Publication Data
Hsuan Hua, 1908-
    Da sheng Bai fa ming men lun qian shi. English/ Shastra
on the door to understanding the hundred dharmas/ by
Vasubandhu Bodhisattva; with commentary by Venerable
Master Hsuan Hua; - 1st ed.
        p. cm.
Includes index.
    ISBN 0-88138-320-7 (soft : alk. paper)
1. Vasubandhu. Mahayanasatadharmaprakasamukhasastra.
I. Vasubandhu. Mahayanasatadharmaprakasamukhasastra.
English. II. Title.

    BQ3080.M327H7813 2004
    294.3'444~dc22

                                        2004001394

by

Vasubandhu Bodhisattva
with commentary of
- Tripitaka Master Hua -

BTTS

Table of Contents

THE SHASTRA ON THE DOOR TO UNDERSTANDING THE HUNDRED DHARMAS

COMPOSED BY
VASUBANDHU BODHISATTVA

TRANSLATED BY
TRIPITAKA MASTER XUAN ZANG OF THE TANG DYNASTY

As the World Honored One has said, "All dharmas have no self." What are "all dharmas," and what is meant by "having no self"? All dharmas may be generally grouped into five categories.

    I. Mind Dharmas (*citta-dharmah*).
    II. Dharmas Belonging to the Mind (*chaitasika-dharmah*).
    III. Form Dharmas (*rupa-dharmah*).
    IV. Activities Dharmas Non-interactive with the Mind (*citta-viprayukta-samskara-dharmah*).
    V. Unconditioned Dharmas (*asamskrita-dharmah*).

They are in this sequence because the first are supreme, the second interact with the first, the third are the shadows manifest by the previous two, the fourth are separate from the positions of the previous three, and the fifth are revealed by the previous four.

The first, Mind Dharmas, include in general eight:

    1. the eye consciousness (*cakshur-vijnana*);
    2. the ear consciousness (*shrotra-vijnana*);
    3. the nose consciousness (*ghrana-vijnana*);
    4. the tongue consciousness (*jihva-vijnana*);
    5. the body consciousness (*kaya-vijnana*);
    6. the mind consciousness (*mano-vijnana*);
    7. the *manas* consciousness (*manas-vijnana*); and,
    8. the *alaya* consciousness (*alaya-vijnana*).

The second, Dharmas Belonging to the Mind, include, in general, fifty-one. They are grouped into six categories:

    A. Five universally interactive (*sarvatraga*);
    B. Five particular states (*viniyata*);
    C. Eleven wholesome (*kushala*);
    D. Six fundamental afflictions (*klesha*);
    E. Twenty derivative afflictions (*upaklesha*); and,
    F. Four unfixed (*aniyata*).

One, the five universally interactive are:

    1. attention (*manaskara*);
    2. contact (*sparsha*);
    3. feeling (*vedana*);
    4. thinking (*samjna*); and,
    5. deliberation (*cetana*).

Two, the five particular states are:

    1. desire (*chanda*);
    2. resolution (*adhimoksha*);
    3. recollection (*smriti*);
    4. concentration (*samadhi*); and,
    5. judgment (*prajna*).

Three, the eleven wholesome dharmas are:

1. faith (*shraddha*);
2. vigor (*virya*);
3. remorse (*hri*);
4. shame (*apatrapya*);
5. absence of greed (*alobha*);
6. absence of anger (*advesha*);
7. absence of foolishness (*amoha*);
8. light ease (*prashrabdhi*);
9. non-laxness (*apramada*);
10. renunciation (*upeksha*); and,
11. non-harming (*ahimsa*).

Four, the six fundamental afflictions are:

1. greed (*raga*);
2. anger (*pratigha*);
3. foolishness (*moha*);
4. arrogance (*mana*);
5. doubt (*vichikitsa*); and,
6. improper views (*drishti*).

Five, the twenty derivative afflictions are:

1. wrath (*krodha*);
2. hatred (*upanaha*);

3. rage (*pradasa*);
4. covering (*mraksha*);
5. deceit (*maya*);
6. flattery (*shathya*);
7. conceit (*mada*);
8. harming (*vihimsa*);
9. jealousy (*irshya*);
10. stinginess (*matsarya*);
11. lack of remorse (*ahrikya*);
12. lack of shame (*anapatrapya*);
13. lack of faith (*ashraddhaya*);
14. laziness (*kausidya*);
15. laxness (*pramada*);
16. torpor (*styana*);
17. restlessness (*auddhatya*);
18. distraction (*mushitasmriti*);
19. improper knowledge (*asamprajanya*); and,
20. scatteredness (*vikshepa*).

Six, the four unfixed are:

1. sleep (*middha*);
2. regret (*kaukritya*);
3. investigation (*vitarka*); and,
4. examination (*vichara*).

The third is the Form Dharmas. In general, there are eleven kinds:

1. eyes (*cakshus*);
2. ears (*shrotra*);
3. nose (*ghrana*);
4. tongue (*jihva*);
5. body (*kaya*);
6. forms (*rupa*);
7. sounds (*shabda*);
8. smells (*gandha*);
9. flavors (*rasa*);
10. objects of touch (*sprashtavya*); and,
11. dharmas pertaining to form (*dharmayatanikani-rupani*).

The fourth is Activities Dharmas Non-interactive with the Mind. In general, there are twenty-four:

1. attainment (*prapti*);
2. life-faculty (*jivitendriya*);
3. generic similarity (*nikaya-sabhaga*);
4. dissimilarity (*visabhaga*);
5. the No-thought Samadhi (*asamjnisamapatti*);
6. the Samadhi of Extinction (*nirodhasamapatti*);
7. the Reward of No-Thought (*asamjnika*);
8. bodies of nouns (*namakaya*);
9. bodies of sentences (*padakaya*);

10. bodies of phonemes (*vyanjanakaya*);
11. birth (*jati*);
12. dwelling (*sthiti*);
13. aging (*jara*);
14. impermanence (*anityata*);
15. revolving (*pravritti*);
16. distinction (*pratiniyama*);
17. interaction (*yoga*);
18. speed (*java*);
19. sequence (*anukrama*);
20. time (*kala*);
21. direction (*desha*);
22. numeration (*samkhya*);
23. combination (*samagri*); and,
24. discontinuity (*anyathatva*).

The fifth is the Unconditioned Dharmas, of which there are, in general, six:

1. unconditioned empty space (*akasha*);
2. unconditioned extinction attained by selection
   (*pratisamkhyanirodha*);
3. unconditioned extinction that is unselected
   (*apratisamkhyanirodha*);

4. unconditioned unmoving extinction (*aninjya*);
5. unconditioned extinction of feeling and thinking (*samjnavedayitanirodha*); and,
6. unconditioned True Thusness (*tathata*).

What is meant by there being no self? There are, in general, two kinds of Non-self: one, the Non-self of Pudgala, and two, the Non-self of Dharmas.

INTRODUCTION

Shastra

The Shastra on the Door to
Understanding the Hundred
Dharmas.

Commentary

The Dharma spoken by the Buddha constitutes the Sutras, the precepts which the Buddha established make up the Vinaya, and the writings of the patriarchs are called the Shastras. Sutras reveal the study of *samadhi*, Vinaya texts disclose the study of precepts, and Shastras discuss the study of wisdom. You could say this is the first time since the founding of the Buddhist Lecture Hall here in San Francisco that a *shastra* is being thoroughly explained. Although we have had classes on *shastras* before, the explanations have been quite simple. This explanation will go into more depth. A lecture series like this is very rare in the West, which is why when people in the West wish to learn to understand *shastras*, there is almost no opportunity to do so. But if people do not understand the Shastras, they will not be able to cultivate. If they cannot cultivate, they will not become Buddhas. And if they do not become Buddhas, they will revolve forever on the wheel of rebirth, being born then dying, and after dying being reborn. When born, people are completely muddled and do not know what happened; and at the time of death they are just about to understand, but time will not wait for them. They die just as muddled, and much as they would like to understand, there is no more time. The reason they do not understand is that they have not investigated **The Shastra on the Door to Understanding the Hundred Dharmas**, and so they are born muddled and die confused over and over again as they turn in the six paths of the revolving wheel. And so now we are lecturing this Shastra.

Someone may ask, "What is *The Shastra on the Door to Understanding the Hundred Dharmas?* Not only have I never seen it, I've never even heard of it before."

That is good. You speak very honestly. When you know, you say you know; and, when you do not know, you say you do not. That means you can still be taught. The trouble is that many people tend to say they know something when they do not in fact know it. If one does not know something but says one does in an attempt to fool people, one is actually only fooling oneself. Someone who claims to know what he does not know, and denies knowing what he does know, is the most foolish kind of person. An example would be if you have never heard of *The Shastra on the Door to Understanding the Hundred Dharmas,* but when someone asks you if you are familiar with it you reply, "Oh, I know that one." Then, when asked what the Shastra discusses you say, "Oh, I've forgotten." That is a clear-cut case of a person saying he knows what he does not in fact know, saying he has mastered what he has not mastered, saying he understands what he does not understand, and claiming to be perfectly clear about what is not at all clear to him. That is the stupidest thing a person can do, and it leads to rebirth as a pig. People who get reborn as pigs were great pretenders in their former lives and acted as though they knew absolutely everything. That is why I feel such pity for pigs when I encounter them. I tell them, "You are lamentable. You just wouldn't listen to instructions in the least. You didn't rely upon the Dharma to cultivate, and so you've fallen into the bodies of pigs."

There are not merely one hundred dharmas; there are 660 dharmas. But there are not merely 660 dharmas; there are actually 84,000 dharmas. The Buddha set forth 84,000 Dharma-doors, and every door is a path to accomplishing Buddhahood. Later on, because living beings' basic natures were too obtuse, 84,000 Dharma-doors became too many. Therefore, Maitreya Bodhisattva very compassionately composed the *Yogacharyabhumi Shastra* (T. 1579), which consolidated the 84,000 Dharma-doors into 660 dharmas. But 660 dharmas were still many, and just to clearly remember their names took several years of effort. Then Vasubandhu, "Heavenly Relative," Bodhisattva contemplated and saw that people in the future whose natures were suited to the Great Vehicle would prefer abbreviation. So he selected the one hundred most important leading dharmas from the *Yogacharyabhumi Shastra's* 660 dharmas and condensed them into *The Shastra on the Door to Understanding the Hundred Dharmas*. That way, all people in the world with dispositions suited to the Great Vehicle could easily remember and understand its dharmas, and no longer have to spend several years just to remember their names. The most obtuse person could memorize these Dharma-doors in an hour, and the smartest person could understand all one hundred dharmas in as little as ten minutes. Would you not call that fast? If you understand these hundred dharmas, you can use them to enter the door of the Buddhadharma. That is why it is called the "Door to Understanding."

Before explaining *The Shastra on the Door to Understanding the Hundred Dharmas*, I would first like to level a criticism. [Note: the year was 1970.] From what I have seen and heard of people in the West who explain the Buddhadharma, if you were to ask them what *The Shastra on the Door to Understanding the Hundred Dharmas* is, what reply would they give? They would not say a word. Now, that would definitely not be as when Manjushri Bodhisattva asked Upasaka Vimalakirti what truth in the primary sense was, and Upasaka Vimalakirti did not say anything at all. His not speaking was in itself truth in the primary sense. If he had spoken, truth in the primary sense would have vanished. So he really did express truth in the primary sense by his silence. But the hundred dharmas are not the same as truth in the primary sense. They must be spoken. If instead of speaking, a person closed his mouth, closed his eyes, and put on a big show of studying truth in the primary sense, that person would be wrong. That is because the very fact that there are one hundred kinds of dharmas means they have to be expressed. Without speaking, there is no way to represent those hundred dharmas.

There are those who profess to be teachers of Dharma but who do not really know how to expound upon a single dharma, not to speak of a hundred. Since they cannot explain even one, they have nothing to say. All they can do is go into some kind of tight-lipped, mystic-eyed trance. Wouldn't you say that was sad? But although there is not a single dharma they understand or speak, still they go outside the hundred dharmas to talk about "Dharma" left and right, up and down. And people who do not understand the Buddhadharma say, "That person can really speak Dharma." But as soon as people who already understand the Buddhadharma hear him, they say, "What is that nonsense all about? He is just singing a song."

This is as when a counterfeiter takes his counterfeit money to the countryside and passes it off to people who cannot tell it is not real, but later at the mint, the officials can see right away that the hallmarks and serial numbers are completely wrong and that the money is phony. It is proved false when compared to the true. In the same way, it may be "Dharma" spoken, but you have to have the Dharma-selecting eye to tell Dharma from non-Dharma and to distinguish which are defiled and which are pure dharmas, which are wholesome and which are unwholesome dharmas, which are deviant and which are proper dharmas. If you know, then you have the Dharma-selecting eye. It should not be that if someone speaks "Dharma" in a booming voice, or sings it like a wailing chant, you become so confused you could not sleep even if you wanted to. Wouldn't you say that was pathetic?!

EXPLANATION OF THE TITLE

Since I cannot sing, I will talk a bit. The hundred dharmas are derived like this: one becomes ten, and ten become one hundred. The hundred dharmas divide into:

I. Eleven Form Dharmas.
II. Eight Mind Dharmas.
III. Fifty-one Dharmas Belonging to the Mind.
IV. Twenty-four Activities Dharmas Not Interactive with the Mind.
V. Six Unconditioned Dharmas.

Each kind in each of these categories will be explained in the Shastra proper. They will not be explained in detail now, during the explanation the title. If we explained them thoroughly right now, there would be nothing to discuss when we got to the Shastra. So, now the kinds and numbers of each are mentioned, and if you understand all about them from that, then you do not have to come back to listen further. But if you do not understand what they are all about yet, then you will have to continue to listen more about them.

People will go home wondering, "What did he mean by eleven kinds of form dharmas, and eight kinds of mind dharmas? That Dharma Master just brought up their names, but he did not tell us anything about them. I really do not want to go back and listen again; but then, there will always remain in my mind this matter that I never got clear about. I'm going to have to go listen."

So now you see why, when introducing the title, we do not go into detail. That is logical enough, wouldn't you say?

Someone who lectures on the Sutras and Shastras has to have a pattern to his talks. He has to have good timing. Then there will be no way for those seriously interested in hearing the Shastra to fail to come and listen. If, of course, the person has the attitude, "I'm not the least bit interested in learning what you mean by a hundred dharmas, or a thousand dharmas or a million dharmas. I don't even care about a single dharma," then there is nothing to be said. But if you are someone who would like to understand the Buddhadharma, then you are definitely going to want to come and listen.

"Door to Understanding" means not being confused, not being muddled, and not being ignorant. It means clarity, clarity about the path of these hundred Dharma-doors, which enable one to cultivate.

"Shastra" is a Sanskrit word that means discussion, discourse. We can use that interpretation here and say that this explanation of the Shastra is also a discussion, and that anyone who does not agree with the way I explain it can bring up his or her own theories, and we will discuss them. That means, if you have questions, I can answer you. A discourse refers to an expression of one's principles. You say what yours are, and I say what mine are, and then we can discuss them and investigate the Dharma. However, the Dharma I speak is not *my* Dharma. What I express is the Buddhadharma. If anyone thinks that I am speaking incorrectly, all you have to do is bring up your reasons, and we will investigate them. I can meet any of your objections. You can come at me with objections, and I can answer them all. That includes all the people in the entire world, no matter what their nationality. Anyone at all can bring up his or her principles, and we will hold a huge symposium. I can answer any question put by any person throughout the ten directions.

"Aha!" you wonder. "How can people come from the ten directions? I can see them coming from four directions or eight directions, but from ten?" Well, now we have airplanes, so suppose someone lands right here in a helicopter, he has come from the upper direction, right? And someone out of a submarine from the sea is equivalent to coming out of the earth, right? So I say again, anyone throughout the ten directions can ask any question they want and we will hold a large symposium to discuss the Buddhadharma. It makes no difference what religion they subscribe to—Buddhism or any other. If they have a question, they can come and ask it. If they have some difficulty, I will use my sword of wisdom to slice right through it for them. I will slice out their tongues, if need be. Then they will not be able to say anything more. You should be clear about this, however. I will slice out their tongues of foolishness, leaving their tongues of wisdom. I will remove their tongues of foolishness and replace them with tongues of wisdom. I am capable of making tongue transplants, as well as brain transplants. If their brains are unclear, I can give them a new set.

Now we will discuss the word "*shastra*." You will remember I said before that the hundred dharmas must be expressed. Why is that? If they were not expressed, there would be no *shastras*. Shastras are discussions of which there are five types.

⊞ Five Kinds of Discussions in Shastras ⊞

1. Right and wrong.
2. Deviant and proper.
3. Good and evil.
4. Cause and effect.
5. Defilement and purity.

First of all, they distinguish what is right and what is wrong. Right is right, and wrong is definitely wrong. One must not take what is right as wrong, nor should one take what is wrong as right. So we discuss things, and in this way come to understand them clearly. For people who enter monastic life, cultivation is right, and failing to cultivate is wrong.

The second thing that *shastras* discuss is what is deviant and what is proper. What is deviant is definitely deviant, and what is proper is decidedly proper. You must not take what is deviant and consider it to be proper, nor take what is proper and consider it to be deviant. That is another reason why there must be discussions. The third reason for discussions is to distinguish good from evil. Good is good, and evil is evil. You cannot regard what is good as being evil, nor regard what is evil as being good.

The fourth function of *shastras* is to discuss cause and effect. A cause is decidedly a cause, and an effect is definitely an effect. You cannot call a cause an effect, nor an effect a cause. You must make your discriminations clearly.

The fifth aspect of *shastras* is to clarify defilement and purity. Defilement is defilement, and purity is purity. You must not take defilement to be purity nor take purity to be defilement. You must not be upside down. And so the function of *shastras* is to discriminate these clearly.

However, it is true that right can turn into wrong, and wrong can become right. If you get rid of what is wrong, then you are right. If you dispense with what is right, you are wrong. The other four meanings also contain this qualification.

Shastras have the above five functions and are thus able to delineate dharmas quite precisely. We can also say, however, that the right is not apart from the wrong and vice-versa. What is right is wrong; what is wrong is right. What is good is just evil, and what is evil is just good. What is deviant is itself proper; what is proper is itself deviant. What is cause is just effect; what is effect is just cause. What is defilement is just purity; what is purity is just defilement. So now you see that when it comes to discussion, you can discuss things any way you want. It is just to be feared you do not have anything to discuss. You say right is wrong and wrong is right? Well, let us see how you explain that. That is the way questions are investigated. "How is it done?" you ask. If you do not know, then you have to study. After you study you will know it yourself. That is the wonder of it. If you only know a little Buddhadharma, you cannot recognize that there is a lot of it. But if you know a lot of it, you cannot say there is only a little. This has been a general explanation of the title: *The Shastra on the Door to Understanding the Hundred Dharmas*. Discussion finished!

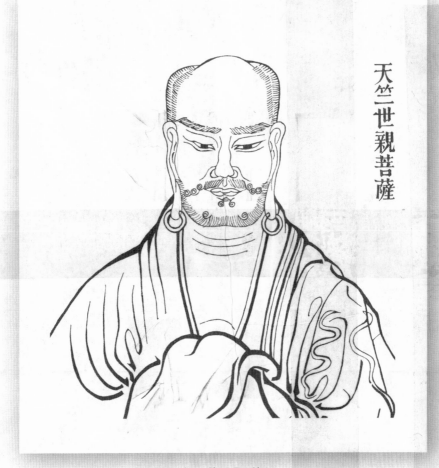

天竺世親菩薩

Vasubandhu Bodhisattva

THE AUTHOR

Shastra

Composed by Vasubandhu
Bodhisattva.

Commentary

This Shastra was **composed by Vasubandhu Bodhisattva,** whose given name translates as "Heavenly Relative" and also as "The Lord's Relative". Some say that he was the younger brother of Lord God. There is really no need to try and research this; people just take it on faith. Vasubandhu Bodhisattva had two brothers. Vasubandhu was their family name. His elder brother's name was Asanga, which means "Unattached." "Heavenly Relative" was the second-born, and the youngest of the three was named Virinchivatsa. "Virinchi" was their mother's name, and *vatsa* is the Sanskrit word which means "son of," and so he was known as "the son of Virinchi". But this brother is too young to come into our present discussion, other than to be introduced to you. All three of these brothers were extremely intelligent. They lived about nine hundred years after the Buddha entered Nirvana. Although they were intelligent, each initially held his own prejudiced view. Later on, they gave up their prejudices.

To begin with, the eldest brother wanted to be "unattached," and although he had no attachments, he preferred the Great Vehicle Buddhadharma. Heavenly Relative was attached to Small Vehicle Buddhadharma. He felt that it was the true Buddhadharma, and he not only studied it, but aided those involved in Small Vehicle Buddhism in berating and slandering the Great Vehicle.

Even though his older brother studied Great Vehicle Buddhism, Heavenly Relative still said it was not true and that the Buddha had not spoken any such Dharma. He did not believe the *Dharma Flower Sutra*, the *Shurangama Sutra*, the *Flower Adornment Sutra*, or any Great Vehicle Buddhism. He, in fact, became a specialist in undermining Great Vehicle Dharma. And so, here we have two brothers, the elder of whom studied Great Vehicle Dharma but did not criticize the Small Vehicle at all, and the younger of whom studied the Small Vehicle, criticized and tried to destroy the Great Vehicle. They did not actually fight, because the contention was only on the part of Heavenly Relative. The whole reason that the Great Vehicle is called by that name is because Great Vehicle Buddhadharma can even include within it that which is incorrect. But the Small Vehicle cannot include what is not correct within it. That is why it is so small. The Great Vehicle can include what is correct and what is incorrect. So, no matter how many offenses his younger brother had, Asanga did not hold them against him, but he did want to save him.

What method did Asanga use to save Heavenly Relative? He wrote his younger brother saying, "Although we do not study the same teachings, still, our relationship as brothers is a fact. We are close relatives for sure, and we both acknowledge this true relationship which exists between us. Now, I know that I am going to die pretty soon, and I would like to see you. This is especially so because I would like your help in doing something, and I believe that you will fulfill my wish in spite of everything. If you do not do this for me, then when I die, I will not be able to close my eyes." Notice that he did not say he was dying, but said, "when I die," leaving the time unfixed.

How could a younger brother not respond to such a sincere letter? Even though they studied two different teachings, Heavenly Relative decided he should go visit his brother Asanga. When he got there he asked what it was his elder brother wished him to do so that Asanga would be able to close his eyes when he died. Asanga said, "I would like you to help me recite the *Dharma Flower Sutra*, the *Shurangama Sutra*, and the *Flower Adornment Sutra*. I would like you to read each one of them to me." That was the method he chose, because he knew his younger brother was extremely intelligent and never forgot anything he read.

Thereupon, Heavenly Relative, in order to fulfill his elder brother's last wish, proceeded to do something that he really did not want to do. He read those three Great Vehicle Sutras aloud for his brother Asanga. When he had finished reading the *Dharma Flower Sutra*, the *Shurangama Sutra*, and the *Avatamsaka*, he knew that he had been completely wrong in the past for criticizing and berating the Great Vehicle Buddhadharma and slandering the Great Vehicle Sutras. He had gone about saying that those Sutras were inauthentic. He now knew how mistaken he had been, and he felt tremendous regret. He became a bit frantic thinking, "What shall I do? I've spent so much time and energy on slandering the Great Vehicle Buddhadharma. It's for sure those offenses will cause me to fall into the hells. There's no question about it. What a despicable tongue I have!" whereupon, he grabbed a knife and was bent upon cutting out his own tongue.

Why did I say earlier that I would cut out people's tongues: their dumb tongues, their dull-witted tongues, their stupid tongues? It is just because Heavenly Relative Bodhisattva himself wanted to slice out his own tongue. He wanted to get rid of his stupid tongue. Anyway, you can imagine the tenseness of the situation. Heavenly Relative had his tongue pulled out and the knife poised over it, ready to lay the blow. It was no joking matter. He was really going to do it. At that point his elder brother, "Unattached," said soothingly, "Second brother, what are you doing? How about telling me what you're up to?"

Heavenly Relative said, "My offenses are too great. I've been continually slandering the Great Vehicle Buddhadharma. Now upon reading those three Sutras, I know that the doctrines of the Great Vehicle are incomparably wonderful. My slander of the Great Vehicle is going to put me in the 'Hell of Pulling Out Tongues,' is it not? So I will just cut out my own tongue right now while I am still alive. What do you think of this idea?" He asked his elder brother's advice.

"Unattached" replied, "Don't be so foolish. You can exchange your tongue." "What do you mean? How?" asked the distraught Heavenly Relative.

"Before, you used your tongue to slander; now, you can use it to praise Great Vehicle Sutras. All you have to do is change your way of talking. That's a much more positive way of going about it. There's no need to cut your tongue out."

Hearing that, Heavenly Relative thought, "He's right. If I cut out my tongue, of what use will that be to Great Vehicle Buddhism? I'll change and praise Great Vehicle Buddhism with it, instead."

As soon as he had that thought, Heavenly Relative's inherent wisdom manifested, and he then composed *The Shastra on the Door to Understanding the Hundred Dharmas*. And so he was a person who changed his faults. He had courageous spirit and valiantly changed what was wrong with him. When he said he was going to change, he actually did it. And after that, all the books he wrote were in praise of the Great Vehicle. He destroyed all the books he had previously written, and the Shastras he wrote in praise of the Great Vehicle circulated all over the world. That is the story, in brief, of Vasubandhu.

Bodhisattva is a Sanskrit word. **Bodhi** means enlightenment; **sattva** means sentient being:

⊞ Two Meanings of Bodhisattva ⊞

1. Enlightener of sentient beings. The Bodhisattva takes the enlightenment that he has testified to, the wisdom that he has opened, and uses that enlightened wisdom to enlighten all other beings who have sentience.
2. An enlightened sentient being. The Bodhisattva is also a sentient being, but he is one who has become enlightened.

Together, these two meanings show that a Bodhisattva is an enlightened sentient being who enlightens other sentient beings. That is the meaning of "Bodhisattva".

"Bodhisattva" is a pretty good name to have, and so lots of people want to give themselves that title. They want others to call them by that name. In China, monastics call each other "Bodhisattva," as a form of mutual praise. But "Bodhisattva" is a title that should be bestowed upon one. It is not that people decide they deserve the title and then give themselves that name. On the other hand, there was Great Master Tai Shu, who said, "All people should call me 'Bodhisattva' instead of 'bhikshu'. Why? I received both the Bhikshu and the Bodhisattva Precepts at full ordination, and so just as you call me a bhikshu, so should you call me 'Bodhisattva'. But, since I haven't yet become a Buddha, you shouldn't call me a 'Buddha'."

Of course, he was just joking. In fact, Great Master Tai Shu *was* a Bodhisattva, and so whether or not anyone called him that made absolutely no difference. It is just for that reason he was able to joke about it. He was chiding when he said, "You should all call me 'Bodhisattva.'" Similarly, the Living Buddha of Gold Mountain announced that everyone should call him a living Buddha. Both those comments were made in the same spirit.

But in this case, was it that Heavenly Relative, who composed this Shastra, signed his name, "Heavenly Relative Bodhisattva"? No. He just signed his name to the Shastra without adding any titles. Later on, devoted scholars, out of reverence for him, added that title to his name. It was not like Ph.D.'s of today who have that print that title on their calling cards and go about advertising their status. I often say to such people, with no malice intended, "What's so great about a Ph.D.s, anyway? You've got a Ph.D. So what?"

The title itself has no intrinsic value. The point is that if you have what it takes, you do not need to praise yourself. It is better for others to do the praising. The same applies to monastics who add the title "Dharma Master" to their names when printing their cards or introducing themselves, because they like the sound of the title. But that title is not something one gives oneself. Therefore, I am sure that Heavenly Relative Bodhisattva did not add a title to his name. Everyone should look into this. Do not become infatuated with name and fame. It is better to call yourself a dead person or a corpse. Pick a name nobody else wants, and then no one will fight you for it. I believe that is a better solution. It is said:

> The superior person goes without a name.
> The inferior person is fond of titles.

Decide for yourselves which type of person you want to be.

THE TRANSLATOR

慈恩唐三藏玄奘法師

Tripitaka Master Xuan Zang

Shastra

**Translated by Tripitaka Master Xuan
Zang of the Tang Dynasty.**

Commentary

Translated by Tripitaka Master Xuan Zang. Now we will discuss the translator. The Shastra was composed in Sanskrit, the language of India, thus it had to be translated in order to be studied by those of other countries. If it had not been translated, then only Indian people would have been able to understand it, and people of other countries would not have had a chance to learn from it. The person who translated this Sutra, therefore, has a lot of merit and virtue. If because of studying this Shastra we are able to understand all dharmas and rely upon Dharmas to cultivate, we have the translator to thank in part. Thus, to begin we should know who the translator was and what contributions he made to Buddhism.

▥ The Monk from Tang ▥

This Monk was of the Tang Dynasty. His contributions to Buddhism were exceptionally great. It can be said that from ancient times to the present, there has never been anyone who can compare to this Dharma Master in his achievements. His secular surname was Chen. His father was an official, but a poor one. Why did he end up poor? It was because he did not take bribes. He was not after the citizens' money, nor that of the government. He was not like officials these days who always feel they are earning too little money so that, on top of their government salary, they try to get the citizens' hard-earned money as well. Dharma Master Xuan Zang's father did not want money. He remained a poor official his entire life. Even though he was poor, he had a virtuous nature. And because of that, among his several children he had two sons who became monks. Dharma Master Xuan Zang's elder brother was a monk who lectured on sutras and was an adept cultivator of his time.

Dharma Master Xuan Zang became a monk and commenced his study of the Buddhadharma at the age of thirteen. During those early years of study, any time a Dharma Master lectured on a Buddhist text, no matter who the Dharma Master was or how far away the lecture was being held, he was sure to go to listen. Whether it was a *sutra* lecture, a *shastra* lecture, or a *vinaya* lecture, he went to listen to them all. Wind and rain could not keep him away from lectures on the Tripitaka, to the point that he even forgot about being hungry. He simply consumed the Dharma, taking the Buddhadharma as his food and drink. He did this for five years, and then he received the Complete Precepts.

However, the principles he had heard Dharma Masters lecturing on during those five years were all different. They all explained the same Sutras in very different ways, each with his own interpretation. And there was a big difference between the lectures of those with wisdom and those without wisdom. But Dharma Master Xuan Zang had not yet really opened enlightenment and he did not have the Dharma-selecting Eye, so how could he know whose lectures to rely on? At that time he vowed to go to India, saying, "The Buddhadharma was transmitted from India, and so there is certainly true and genuine Buddhadharma to be found in India."

Thereupon, he wrote a request for permission to go to India to seek the Dharma, and presented it to the Emperor. The Emperor Tai Zong of the Tang Dynasty did not grant his wish. But Dharma Master Xuan Zang, who was already resolved to go, said, "I would prefer to disobey the Son of Heaven and have my head cut off than not to go to India seeking the Dharma."

So he returned to the monastery and began to practice mountain climbing. He piled chairs, tables, and benches together to simulate mountains, and practiced jumping from one piece of furniture to the next. That was his method of practicing mountain climbing. From morning until night he leaped from table to chair. Probably there were not any big mountains where he lived, so he had to practice in the temple. All the young, middle-aged, and elder novices wondered what he was up to, jumping on furniture all day long instead of reciting *sutras* or cultivating. He did not tell anyone that he was training to climb the Himalayas, so most people thought he was playing. Eventually he trained his body so that it was very strong, and then when he was physically able, he started his trip through Siberia.

On the day of his departure, when the Emperor Tai Zong learned that he intended to go even without Imperial consent, the Emperor asked him, "I have not given you permission, and you still insist on going. When will you be back?"

Dharma Master Xuan Zang replied, "Look at that pine tree. The needles are pointing toward the west. When those needles turn around and face east, I will return."

He did not say how many years that would be. So he set out. At that time there were no airplanes, steamboats, buses, or trains. There were boats, but they were made of wood and were not too sturdy. Furthermore, since he did not have Imperial permission, he probably could not have gotten the use of a boat anyway. So he traveled by land through many countries, from the Siberian area of the Russian border to India. He was gone for more than a decade. When he reached India, he did not know the language at all. But gradually he studied Sanskrit, and over time he listened to many Indian Dharma Masters lecture on the Buddhadharma. Some people say this took him fourteen years. Others say it took nineteen. In general, he went through a great deal of suffering and difficulty to study the Buddhadharma and then, when he had completed his studies, he returned to China.

When his return was imminent, the needles on the pine tree turned to the east. As soon as the Emperor saw that the pine needles were indeed pointing east, he knew that Dharma Master Xuan Zang was returning, and he sent out a party of officials to the western gate to welcome and escort him back. When they reached the gate, there, indeed, was Dharma Master Zang returning.

Dharma Master Xuan Zang then concentrated on translating the Sutras and other works that he had brought back with him. He translated from Sanskrit to Chinese. When he was translating the *Great Prajna Sutra* the peach trees blossomed six times within that one single year. That was a sign of the auspiciousness of the Great *Prajna Sutra* and its importance to all of us. The fact that it was being translated moved even the wooden trees and plants to display their delight.

Dharma Master Xuan Zang translated a great many *sutras*. While in India, he bowed to the Buddha's *sharira*, his relics, teeth and bones. He saw where the Buddha in a previous life had sacrificed his eyes, and went to the place where the Buddha in a previous life had sacrificed his head. He visited the location where the Buddha in a former life had practiced the conduct of patience, and went to the site where the Buddha in a previous incarnation had given up his body for the sake of a tiger. He also went to see the Bodhi tree under which the Buddha had sat and accomplished the Way. He went to all of those places celebrated in Buddhism. Those pilgrimages are another indication of the extent of his true sincerity. While in India, whenever he met Dharma Masters, he never looked down on them, no matter whether they cultivated or not. He was extremely respectful. He was not the least bit arrogant or haughty. When he finished his studies, many Small Vehicle Dharma Masters and masters of externalist ways came to debate with him, but none was able to defeat him.

Dharma Master Xuan Zang is known as a Tripitaka Master. Tripitaka means "Three Stores, Three Baskets". The Tripitaka includes the Sutra Store, the Shastra Store and the Vinaya Store. He was honored with this title because he understood all three Stores without any obstruction and could explain them all.

⊞ Two Meanings of Dharma Master ⊞

1. One who bestows the Dharma upon people.
2. One who takes the Dharma as his master.

As to his name, Xuan means "esoteric and wonderful". He was esoteric in the sense that none could really understand him. Tsang means "awe-inspiring". He was awe-inspiring in that he could do what others could not do. He was an outstanding person among his peers. His wisdom surpassed all those around him. He is the one who translated this *Shastra on the Door to Understanding the Hundred Dharmas* into Chinese. Because the Dharma Master understood both Chinese and Sanskrit, he did not make mistakes in his translations of the *sutras*, and his translations of *shastras* are even more reliable.

▥ The Three Cart Patriarch ▥

At that time, Dharma Master Xuan Zang had more than eight hundred bhikshus helping him translate the Sutras spoken by the Buddha. They were a group of extremely talented people. The most renowned among them was Dharma Master Kuei Ji. He was known as the "Three Cart Patriarch". Why was he called that? It is because, prior to his becoming a monk, he presented some conditions to the Emperor. His consenting to the imperial edict he had received ordering him to leave domestic life was contingent upon being given three carts. He wanted those three carts to follow him wherever he went. One of these carts was to be filled with wine. Basically monks do not drink wine, but he considered himself special. Another cart was to carry fresh meat, because he liked to eat it. And the third cart had to contain beautiful women. Now you see how he got his nickname. However, you should be clear that the Three Cart Patriarch was not an ordinary person. For one thing, no ordinary person would dare present such conditions to the Emperor when he had been commanded to become a monk. In order to understand how special he was, we have to look into his previous life.

When Dharma Master Xuan Zang was on his way to India, he encountered an old cultivator way up in the mountains. The old cultivator had been meditating there for so long that the dust that had accumulated on his clothing was an inch or more thick. The birds, unafraid, had obviously made a seasonal habit of nesting in his hair. They had built their nests, laid their eggs, and reared their young while he remained there in *samadhi*. It would be hard to say how many years he had been sitting in that same spot unmoving. Anyway, Dharma Master Xuan Zang rang his bell to bring the old cultivator out of *samadhi*. The old fellow came out of *samadhi* all right, but he could not move. He was as stiff as a board, but he was able to ask, "Why did you ring the bell and bring me out of meditation?"

Dharma Master Xuan Zang asked him, "Old cultivator, how long have you been sitting here in *samadhi*? What's the sense of never coming out of meditation?"

The old cultivator replied, "I'm waiting for the Red Yang Buddha to come into the world. Then I'm going to help him propagate the Buddhadharma."

Dharma Master Xuan Zang said, "But the Red Yang Buddha has come and gone already. He entered the world and has already passed into Nirvana. You sat here waiting and didn't even know the Red Yang had arrived and the Red Yang Buddha's Dharma was in the world."

"Well, what era is it?" asked the cultivator, and Dharma Master Xuan Zang related that he was from the Tang Dynasty, and that it was the first year of the Jen Guan reign period. "That's all right," said the cultivator. "If the Red Yang Buddha has come and gone, I'll wait for the White Yang Buddha," and he prepared to re-enter *samadhi*.

Dharma Master Xuan Zang called him back saying something like, "Old Bodhisattva!" or "Dhyana companion!" or "Old cultivator!" Those were the standard forms of address at that time. He said, "Don't re-enter *samadhi*! It would be better if you followed me to help propagate the Buddhadharma. Although Shakyamuni Buddha, the Red Yang Buddha, has already gone to Nirvana, his Dharma is still in the world. Come along and help me spread the teaching."

"How can I help propagate it?" asked the old cultivator.

The Dharma Master said, "You go to Chang An, and when you come to the house with the yellow-tiled roof, get reborn there, and you can eventually help propagate the Dharma." That is because his present physical body was useless, and he would need to trade it in for a new one. "You first go there and get reborn, and when I get back you can help me propagate the Buddhadharma."

The old cultivator thought it over and agreed. So the old cultivator went off to rebirth in Chang An, and Dharma Master Xuan Zang went on his way to India to bring back the *sutras*. When he got back, the first thing he did was congratulate the T'ang Dynasty Emperor Tai Zong on the birth of his son. "I sent you back someone to be your son. That was been a happy event indeed!"

But the Emperor said, "No. I didn't have a son while you were away."

"No?" said the Dharma Master, and he looked into it and realized that the old cultivator had gotten off the track and been reborn in the house of the Defense Minister Yu Chi Gong instead. Yu Chi Gong was tough and had a black face. He was very talented and worked hard at his job, helping the Emperor maintain the country and rule the empire. Probably the old cultivator was a bit sloppy when he did things, so although Dharma Master Xuan Zang had told him clearly to get born in the house with the yellow-tiled roof, the old fellow got it wrong, chose the one with the blue tiles, and ended up becoming the nephew of the flamboyant Defense Minister. Perhaps you can imagine what it was like being the nephew of Yu Chi Gong. As soon as he was old enough, he took a tremendous fancy to eating meat, drinking wine, and entertaining women. Perhaps because he had cultivated for *kalpas*, sitting in *samadhi* without ever coming out, he had had a few false thoughts like, "Meat isn't bad as I recall. And I remember it was pleasant to drink wine. As for women, they weren't bad either." So that when he reincarnated, he could not put down the contents of those three carts.

But as soon as Dharma Master Xuan Zang learned from the Emperor that there was no prince, he checked things out and knew that the old cultivator was in fact Yu Chi Gong's nephew. So he approached the Defense Minister and said, "You know, there's someone in your family whom I sent here to help propagate the Buddhadharma."

The Defense Minister said shortly, "Well, you told him to come, so you tell him to go." Thus was he told; but he would not go.

Finally Dharma Master Xuan Zang related the causes and conditions to Emperor Tai Zong who said immediately, "I'll issue an Imperial Command and order him to leave home."

"Fine," said Master Xuan Zang. "But it's likely he'll want to make it conditional. Whatever conditions he demands, just agree to them."

The Emperor assented, and thereupon commanded the nephew of Yu Chi Gong to appear in court for an audience. "You must leave home," was the Emperor's order. "If I want to leave home I will, and if I don't want to leave home, I won't."

"This is a royal command, and if you don't obey it, you will be beheaded."

That put a scare into the nephew, and so he complied; but he still had the audacity to set up three conditions. "I want a cart of meat, a cart of wine, and a cart of women to follow me wherever I go.

"Agreed," said the Emperor. So it was decided, and the nephew headed for Da Xing Shan, "Great Flourishing Goodness," Monastery to become a monk. Since he was the son of a prominent official, there was quite a fanfare, and as the procession neared the temple gates, the big bell was rung and the gigantic drum was beaten to welcome him. As soon as he heard bell and drum he opened enlightenment and said, "Oh, that's the way it is. To start with I was an old cultivator on that mountain." With a flick of his hand he waved away the carts, "Take them back. I don't want them anymore." But although he dismissed the carts upon leaving home, still people called him "The Three Cart Patriarch."

THE SHASTRA

Shastra

As the World Honored One has said,
"All dharmas have no self."

Commentary

Now we begin the discussion of the Shastra proper. The word "**as**" indicates that what is about to be said is a quote from **the World Honored One** himself. And who is the World Honored One? "World Honored One" is one of the ten titles of a Buddha. It represents how the Buddha is "honored in the world and beyond the world." It is used here instead of the word "Buddha" to enhance the literary quality of the Chinese text, which in general employs four-character phrases.

The Buddha **has said, "All dharmas have no self."** All dharmas must be without a self.

"But why?" you wonder. "The self is truly and actually present, so why is it said there should be no self?"

You say that the self, your own self, is truly and actually present? Let us suppose that is so. But then when you die, the corpse is still your same old body. Where did the self of you go off to? If when you die the self disappears, then how can there actually be a self when you are still alive? There is a problem inherent in your supposition.

The Buddha talked about all dharmas, but qualified it by saying that all dharmas have to be without a self. There should not be a self. You should not be like people who do not understand the Dharma and yet brag, "I spoke such-and-such Dharma, I lectured such-and-such a Sutra," thrusting the self out in front. Recently when we set thirty-six pigeons free, two of them stayed. Why are they pigeons now? It is just because of clinging to a self. Before, when they were people, they did not listen to the Dharma spoken by the Buddha and were unable to be without a self, so they wound up being birds, in the animal realm.

The Shastra begins by quoting the Buddha, saying, "All dharmas have no self." The self referred to here is a view of self. It does not refer one's own body. There should not be any view of self. In the *Vajra Sutra* the Buddha spoke about a view of self, a view of others, a view of living beings and a view of life spans. One should not have any of those views.

Not only should one not have a self, there should not even be any dharmas. All dharmas, as well, do not exist. And if no dharmas exist, even less does a self exist. Because of that, people who cultivate the Way should get to the point of having no self, and then each and every dharma is perfected. If one can truly be without self, then all dharmas interpenetrate without obstruction. Whatever dharma one takes up does not fail to be of the Dharma Realm; each has the nature of the Dharma Realm. And all dharmas then appear before one. Although all dharmas manifest, one should be so there also are no dharmas. The Wonderful is just at that point, and the difficulty is also right at that point. For all dharmas whatsoever to manifest before one, and yet for one to have no attachments to any dharmas, means that one has emptied dharmas of all attributes. There are no attributes of dharmas at all. When one gets to that point, then one really experiences true interpenetration without obstruction, and one obtains incredible freedom and ease. If one can be without self, then one will have freedom; but if one cannot manage to get rid of the self, one will be incapable of being free. Therefore, what is important is not to have a self.

And yet, how can one not have a self? It is not easy. One may think, "Here I am listening to the Shastra being lectured, and how can you tell me that I don't have a self, that I'm not here?"

I repeat, if you can be here listening to the Shastra and yet not know that you are here listening to the Shastra—forgetting about people and having no ego, emptying your self, so there are no people, there is no self and there are no dharmas, so that people and dharmas are both empty—then you will be truly free and at ease. But your attachments keep you from being free of self. What are you attached to? You are attached to the five *skandhas*: form, feeling, thinking, activities, and consciousness. Among the five *skandhas* you reckon the form body, this false self, to be your self. But actually, did I not just point out that when you die it is still your body, but it does not have any awareness, and so where did the self go? Your self is huge-like Mount Sumeru. When you die, where does it go? You do not know. Wouldn't you say that is tragic?

Those of externalist ways are attached to a "great self," a "small self," and a "spiritual self." They have a whole collection of selves. They say the "great self" is such that there is nothing greater, and the "small self" is such that there is nothing smaller. This aspect of their theories has no use. The only useful part is the "spiritual self" in between. That is the "spiritual self" to which those of externalist ways become attached, their attachment being to the "spiritual self"

Those of the Small Vehicle, the Two Vehicles, also have their attachments. They have an attachment to a lopsided view of Nirvana, called a biased view of the self. Bodhisattvas, too, have attachments. What are their attachments? They are attached to the existence of living beings that can be liberated, to a Buddha Way that can be sought, and to a True Thusness to which they certify. Their certification has not reached the point of being without knowing and without attaining. They still have something to which they certify, something that they attain. They certify to and attain True Thusness. Since Bodhisattvas have these attachments, they also have not forgotten the self. They still have a self. And as long as one has a self, one still has falseness. In the Buddhadharma, one wants to be without a self in one's cultivation of all dharmas. Then one can obtain the state of the Great Vehicle.

The Shastra begins with this quotation of what was spoken by the Buddha, that "All dharmas have no self." The subsequent text was written by Heavenly Relative Bodhisattva.

Shastra

What are "all dharmas," and what
is meant by "having no self"? All
dharmas may be generally grouped
into five categories.

Commentary

What are all dharmas, and what is meant by "having no self"? Now Heavenly Relative Bodhisattva will analyze the Buddha's words. **All dharmas may be generally grouped into five categories.** This is looking at them from a broad and comprehensive viewpoint. What are the five categories?

⊞ **The Five Categories** ⊞

I.   The Eight Mind Dharmas.
II. The Fifty-one Dharmas Belonging to the Mind.
III. The Eleven Form Dharmas.
IV. The Twenty-four Activities Dharmas Non-interactive with the Mind.
V.   The Six Unconditioned Dharmas.

Shastra

I. Mind Dharmas

Commentary

The first one, **Mind Dharmas,** refers to dharmas of the Mind King. The mind is called King, because each and every dharma is established based upon the mind. If there were no Mind Dharmas, then no dharmas would exist at all. It is said:

> The Buddha spoke all dharmas for the sake of the minds
> of all living beings.
> If it were not for all those minds, of what use would all
> dharmas be?

There are eight Mind King dharmas, but we will not talk about them yet, as they will be discussed later.

Shastra

II. Dharmas
Belonging to the
Mind.

There are two ways to interpret the second category, **Dharmas Belonging to the Mind**. On the one hand they are Dharmas Belonging to the Mind, and on the other, they are servants of the mind. They work for the mind. The mind is King, and the Dharmas Belonging to the Mind are his servants. But they are also like great ministers. The King is unable to carry out actions himself, so he uses those belonging to the mind to do things. That is the meaning of belonging to the mind. They are also known as enumerations of the mind, because they have a fixed number; there are fifty-one of them. Since these dharmas arise from the mind, they are of the same family as the mind. Hence they are called Dharmas Belonging to the Mind, the second category.

Shastra

III. Form Dharmas.

Commentary

Form Dharmas is the third category. Anything that has form and shape, that has a substantial aspect to it, is known as a form dharma. This does not just refer to their color but also to their tangible form, their substantive aspect. There are eleven Form Dharmas. They, too, will be discussed later on.

Shastra

IV. Activities Dharmas
Non-interactive
With the Mind.

Commentary

Category four, **Activities Dharmas Non-interactive with the Mind,** refers to dharmas that do not interact, do not work together with the dharmas of any of the other categories. These kinds of dharmas are produced on their own from the mind without interacting. They are related to and have aspects of activities. There are twenty-four such dharmas.

Shastra

V. Unconditioned
Dharmas.

Commentary

The previous four categories were all conditioned dharmas. This final category, number five, is that of **Unconditioned Dharmas**. These are dharmas used in cultivation of the world-transcending Great Vehicle. The states they represent can be certified to if one cultivates transcendental dharmas.

We have not said anything in detail about the five categories of dharmas yet, because they will all be discussed in detail later when we come to them in the text.

To review, the first four categories are conditioned dharmas and the fifth is Unconditioned Dharmas. If one only knows about the first four kinds, then one is an ordinary person or an externalist. If one only knows the dharmas of the last category, the Unconditioned Dharmas, then one resides in the one-sided emptiness of the Small Vehicle, which has not reached the state of the Great Vehicle. What is the state of the Great Vehicle?

> Right in the midst of the conditioned is the unconditioned.

It is right within conditioned dharmas that one sees Unconditioned Dharmas. It is not that one leaves conditioned dharmas behind and finds other dharmas that are unconditioned. Rather, its being conditioned or unconditioned just differs by a single thought. Understanding the unconditioned while in the midst of the conditioned is what is meant by "being in the world while transcending the world." Being that way while in the world, one does not fight, is not greedy, has no impeding obstructions, and is free and at ease. One exists in a state of interpenetration, and it is extremely blissful. To be in the world while transcending the world is the state of a Great Vehicle Bodhisattva. If at that point one can progress further and use the principle of selflessness to cultivate courageously and vigorously, then one can obtain the fruition of Wonderful Enlightenment.

This has been an overall view of the Five Categories of Dharmas.

Shastra

They are in this sequence because
the first are supreme, the second
interact with the first, the third are
the shadows manifest by the previous
two, the fourth are separate from the
positions of the previous three, and
the fifth are revealed by the previous
four.

Commentary

They are in this sequence because of the following reasons. **The first** refers to the Mind Dharmas. They **are supreme** over all else, since the mind is king and all dharmas arise from it. **The second interact with the first.** The second category is Dharmas Belonging to the Mind. They obey the orders of the Mind King. **The third are the shadows manifest by the previous two.** Form Dharmas are the third category. Form Dharmas come into being from the shadows cast by the Mind Dharmas and the Dharmas Belonging to the Mind. Therefore, Form Dharmas belong to the marks division of the eighth consciousness.

⊞ **Two Divisions of the Eighth Consciousness** ⊞

1. Seeing division.
2. Marks division.

The marks division basically has no nature of its own. We see all sorts of things as having shape, form, marks, or characteristics, but basically they do not exist at all. It is simply that the eighth consciousness makes them appear.

The fourth are separate from the positions of the previous three. The fourth category is activities dharmas not interactive with the mind. They are separate from Mind Dharmas, Dharmas Belonging to the Mind, and Form Dharmas. **And the fifth are revealed by the previous four.** Those in the fifth category, Unconditioned Dharmas, are extremely profound. There is no way one could understand them. But in order to attempt to understand them, one must make use of the conditioned dharmas. The Unconditioned Dharmas are revealed by the conditioned dharmas.

The categories of the Hundred Dharmas are in this sequence. They go from Mind Dharmas, to Dharmas Belonging to the Mind, to Form Dharmas, to Activities Dharmas Non-interactive with the Mind, to Unconditioned Dharmas. They appear in that order for the reasons just given.

Shastra

The first, Mind Dharmas, include in
general eight:

1. the eye
   consciousness;
2. the ear
   consciousness;
3. the nose
   consciousness;
4. the tongue
   consciousness;
5. the body
   consciousness;
6. the mind
   consciousness;
7. the *manas*
   consciousness; and
8. the *alaya*
   consciousness.

Commentary

Now, at last, we are going to discuss some dharmas. **The first, Mind Dharmas, include in general eight.** One, the **eye consciousness**. We say that eyes can see, but it is not actually the eyes themselves that see. It is the eye consciousness that sees. Two, **the ear consciousness.** We say the ears can hear, but if your ears were sliced off and laid aside, would they be able to hear by themselves? No. If your eyes were gouged and set aside would they be able to see? Could you say, "I'm not going to the movies, but I'll send my eyes along, and they can take in the show." Obviously not. The eyes cannot see by themselves. It is the eye consciousness that does the seeing. And from where does the eye consciousness come? It comes from the mind, the Mind King. The same is true for all the other consciousnesses as well: three, **the nose consciousness;** four, **the tongue consciousness;** five, **the body consciousness;** and six, **the mind consciousness.** The six sense faculties of eyes, ears, nose, tongue, body, and mind combine with the six defiling sense objects of sights, sounds, smells, tastes, objects of touch and dharmas. When that occurs, a consciousness arises between each pair. On the inside there are six faculties, on the outside there are six sense objects, and in the middle, in between the faculties and their objects, the six consciousnesses arise. Taken together, these three sets of six make up the Eighteen Realms. I discussed these in detail when I lectured the *Heart Sutra*, so if you want to further explore them, you can look into that text.

The mind consciousness, the sixth or "intellectual" consciousness, is not actually the substance of the mind. The sixth consciousness is the function of the mind, whose substance is seven, **the** *manas* **consciousness**, also called the "transmitting" consciousness, or the "defiling" consciousness. The seventh consciousness is the substance of the mind. It continually takes the functions of the sixth consciousness and transmits them to the eighth, **the** *alaya* **consciousness**. The eighth consciousness is called the *alaya*, which means "store," because it stores all information transmitted to it by the seventh. If it is turned around, it becomes the Nature of the Treasury of the Thus Come One.

When the eight consciousnesses are turned around, they become four kinds of wisdom.

⊞ Four Kinds of Wisdom ⊞

1. The great perfect mirror wisdom.
2. The wisdom of equality.
3. The wisdom of wonderful contemplation.
4. The wisdom that accomplishes what is done.

How does one turn them around? One must work hard at cultivation, and then one will know how to do it. I cannot tell you now, because even if I were to tell you, in the future you still would not know.

> Upon awakening, one naturally obtains them.

If you yourself cultivate, then you yourself will know. Before you know, it does not do any good to be told. But once you know, you very naturally will have the use of them.

Alaya is a Sanskrit word that means "storehouse." The *alaya* is the store consciousness, because it is like the ground in which we plant seeds, storing them away until they sprout. That is why there are often analogies made likening the mind to the ground or to a field. For instance it is said,

> Plant the ground of the mind;
> Nurture the field of the nature.

All the different external and internal states we experience, whether good or bad, defiled or pure, are planted as seeds in the eighth consciousness. The seeds of every event, circumstance, and experience are stored away in that store consciousness. If you cultivate and turn that store consciousness around, then it becomes the Nature of the Treasury of the Thus Come One. It is just a matter of being able to use it. If you can use it, then the great perfect mirror wisdom will appear. If you cannot use it, then you just keep on having false thinking. And all the false thoughts you have, whether they come about or not, still get stored in the eighth consciousness. Even the most subtle kinds of mental activities, impulses of which you are completely unaware, get stored there as seeds.

> In a single unenlightened thought,
> The three subtle marks appear.

[Note: The Three Subtle Marks are the mark of karma, the mark of turning, and the mark of manifesting.] When they appear, the Thus Come One's Treasury turns into the eighth consciousness. However, if you are able to turn that eighth consciousness back around to become the Nature of the Treasury of the Thus Come One, then you are one who has returned to the origin and gone back to the source.

This has been a general explanation of the Eight Mind Dharmas. When discussed in detail, the subject is quite complex.

Among the Eight Mind Dharmas, the sixth is called the mind consciousness. And why is the seventh also called the *manas*, "mind" or "intellectual" consciousness? It is because the sixth exists in reliance on the seventh consciousness. The seventh is the basis, the fundamental mind consciousness. It is the root of the mind consciousness, whereas the sixth is the function of the mind consciousness. The seventh consciousness is called the "defiled consciousness." It is also known as "that on which defiled and pure rely." The sixth consciousness is defiled, and the eighth consciousness is pure. The purity of the eighth consciousness relies upon the seventh consciousness, hence its name: "that on which defiled and pure rely."

The eighth consciousness is the *alaya* consciousness. Alaya means "non-vanishing," and it also means "store." "Non-vanishing" refers to how True Thusness accords with birth and death and yet remains and does not vanish. True Thusness is never lost; it does not disappear. "Store" consciousness has three meanings.

⊞ **The Three Meanings of Store Consciousness** ⊞

1. That which stores.
2. That which is stored.
3. Attaching and storing.

The first meaning is "that which stores," because it stores all good and evil seeds within it. The second meaning is "that which is stored," referring to the seeds stored in the eighth consciousness. All good and evil karma is stored here. The third meaning is "attaching and storing," for attachment and storing take place within the eighth consciousness.

Absolutely everything we do, every thought we have, be it good or bad, is stored in the eighth consciousness. All dharmas whatsoever are manifestations from the eighth consciousness. The things that we see comprise the marks division of the eighth consciousness. Our ability to see them makes up the seeing division of the eighth consciousness. That is why it is said that the myriad dharmas are consciousness only; they arise from consciousness alone. Consciousness is just True Thusness when it is bound. Consciousness is also what we refer to as the Buddha-nature. It is also the source of all good and evil. And it is the original home, the ancestral village, of all ordinary people and sages.

The second, Dharmas Belonging
to the Mind, include, in general,
fifty-one. They are grouped into six
categories:

    A. Five universally
       interactive;
    B. Five particular
       states;
    C. Eleven wholesome;
    D. Six fundamental
       afflictions;
    E. Twenty derivative
       afflictions; and,
    F. Four unfixed.

One, the five universally interactive are:

1. attention;
2. contact;
3. feeling;
4. thinking; and,
5. deliberation.

Commentary

Now we will discuss **the second, Dharmas Belonging to the Mind**. Dharmas Belonging to the Mind also belong to Mind Dharmas, but they are subjects of the mind, not the Mind King. The Mind King is the eighth consciousness. The Mind King, at the time of direct perception—that is, perception through the nature—pervades the entire Dharma Realm and has no wearisome defilements. It can stop all karmic retribution. But, these Dharmas Belonging to the Mind help the mind enact deeds of good and evil, creating good or evil karma. The Mind King is like an emperor. Just as an emperor orders his ministers to carry out his commands, so, too, the Mind King relies on the Dharmas Belonging to the Mind in order to get things done. In this case, they **include, in general, fifty-one.** They are also known as servants of the mind. Another name for them is enumerations of the mind. The mind has so many of these kinds of deliberations that they could never be counted, but there are fifty-one enumerations of the mind that are most important. **They**—these Fifty-one Dharmas Belonging to the Mind—**are further grouped into six categories.**

These six categories are like departments. The first one is the **five universally interactive dharmas,** which are called that because they pervade all places. They operate universally, and there are five specific dharmas listed in this division. Two is the **five particular states** dharmas; they are independent. Whereas the universally interactive dharmas pervade all places, these particular states do not pervade at all. They are isolated. They are very special, solitary, and exclusive states. There are also five of these listed. Three is the **eleven wholesome** dharmas. Eleven specific ones are listed.

Four, the **six fundamental afflictions**, is the next division. We talk about having afflictions, but now we will learn more specifically just what types of afflictions there are, along with where they come from. The six fundamental afflictions are just six kinds of poison. Division five is the **twenty derivative afflictions**. The six kinds of afflictions just discussed are the basic ones, but there are also subsidiary afflictions, twenty in number. These twenty afflictions are further subdivided into minor, moderate, and strong afflictions. And six, the last division is the **four unfixed Dharmas Belonging to the Mind**.

Now we will begin discussing the first one, the five universally interactive. What are they? The text goes on to explain: One, **attention.** Attention is as when paying attention, putting one's mind's attention on something, or literally "making a mind". Attention is an attempt to grasp onto a state. Basically, the Mind King does not enter into this act of attention by itself. But because of good and evil karma planted as seeds in the eighth consciousness from long-distant past *kalpas* to the present, the eighth consciousness becomes permeated by these habitual tendencies, just as smoke permeates food being cured, or incense permeates the atmosphere of the Buddhahall. When the permeation reaches a saturation point, movement arises within the eighth consciousness. That movement takes the form of attention. Therefore, attention marks the beginning of the mind giving rise to a state.

The situation of a Bodhisattva is such that he is omniscient without having to perform the act of attention. He can know good and evil, causes and effects without making an effort to do so. Arhats, however, do have to perform the act of attention. They must pay attention to see what is going on. Once they have gone through the process of attention, then they can know what something is all about. They can know the causes and results of any given situation that occurs.

For example, why did the thirty-four pigeons fly away? Basically, it is because when they were people they created certain kinds of karma. They did not work hard at their cultivation. They thought they would leave home, but they never did. They thought they would get around to cultivating, but they never did. They thought they would become vegetarians, but they never did. They thought they would recite the Buddha's name, but they never did. They never got around to doing what they were supposed to be doing.

This does not apply just to pigeons. Some people who come to the Buddhist Lecture Hall never leave. Others come but do not stay. Still others intend to come but never make it in the door. You should not look upon these conditions as ordinary, nothing special, and take them for granted. They are, in fact, quite extraordinary. People without good roots simply cannot get themselves inside the door of the Buddhist Lecture Hall. If the people here did not have good roots, they would not be able to listen to *sutra* lectures. All those who are able to listen to *sutra* lectures have good roots. However, even then, there are great good roots and small good roots; there are those with many good roots and those with few good roots. If you want to bring forth the resolve for Bodhi, you must listen to more and more Dharma lectures. When you come to understand a lot of Buddhadharma, then very naturally, you will resolve your mind on Bodhi. That is what is meant by attention.

Attention is universally interactive, and the second universally interactive dharma, is **contact**, which is also what the remaining three universally interactive dharmas—**feeling, thinking, and deliberation**—rely upon. Once contact is established, feeling arises. Once feeling arises, there is thinking, and then there is deliberation. Therefore, contact provides the locus for feeling, thinking, and deliberation to base themselves upon.

Contact is not something you should want. As soon as you have reached the state of contact, there will be feeling belonging to the mind, thinking belonging to the mind, and deliberation belonging to the mind. With attention, as mentioned above, comes the start of a state arising from the mind. However, with contact comes the start of a mind arising from the state, a kind of mental false thought. As a false thought of the mind arises, then a mental attitude of feeling is produced toward the state. There is a drive to experience the feeling, which is thinking; thinking about the state and then pursuing it. Therefore, the false thinking is produced from the state. Once there is thinking, then there will be deliberation. What is deliberation? Deliberation captures the mind, causing the mind to take stock, to calculate and reckon: "How can I get that state? What can I do?"

The World Nature of True Suchness

The Eight Consciousness

THE SEEING DIVISION

THE MARKS DIVISION

THE SEVENTH
CONSCIOUSNESS
(Transmitting/Defiling)

THE SIXTH
CONSCIOUSNESS
(Mind/Intellect)

THE FIVE SENSE ORGANS
(Inner Faculties)

CONSCIOUSNESS 1-5
(Sense Perception)

THE FIVE
UNIVERSALLY ACTIVE

THE SIX SENSE ORGANS
(External States)

The Five Universally Active

THE BEGINNING OF
THE MIND GIVING
RISE TO STATES

1. Attention

(simultaneous)

2. Contact

3. Feeling
   (Sensation, Reception, Preception—
   experienced as pleasurable, painful, or
   neutral; can also add the experience by
   the sixth consciousness, making five)

4. Conceptualization
   (Congnition, Thought, Mental
   Recognition of a State)

5. Deliberation
   (Thought that will lead to the Five
   Particular States)

STOP THE CREATION
OF GOOD AND EVIL
KARMA
BY APPLYING EFFORT

The five just discussed are called the five universally interactive. They are universally interactive because they pervade the three natures and extend throughout the three periods of time.

⊞ The Three Moral Aspects ⊞

1. The good nature.
2. The evil nature.
3. The indeterminate nature.

"Indeterminate" means it is not known whether it is good or evil.

⊞ The Three Periods of Time ⊞

1. Past.
2. Present.
3. Future.

These are also referred to as past time, present time, and future time, covering all times. What is meant by "past"? What is meant by "present"? What is meant by "future"? I will tell you. Today is the present, yesterday was the past, and tomorrow is the future. The future does not exist, because it has not come. The present keeps changing and does not stay still, so it does not exist either. The past is already gone, and so it does not exist. Therefore, although the five universally interactive dharmas pervade the three periods of time, ultimately they cannot be got at.

If one could put a stop to the five kinds of universally interactive dharmas—which one *could* do whenever one wanted—then one would not create evil karma. But if you do not stop them, they continue to exist. Actually, with the coming into being of the five universally interactive dharmas, one still has not created any good or evil karma. It is when the five particular states arise that there is no stopping the creation of good and evil karma.

Two, the five particular states are:

1. desire;
2. resolution;
3. recollection;
4. concentration;
   and,
5. judgment.

Commentary

"Particular" can have several meanings, such as "special," "distinct," and "individual". The word "particular" is used to describe these dharmas as different from the five universally interactive. Each one of the five universally interactive dharmas includes the meanings of all five. But **the five particular states** are not the same as each other and are, in fact, quite distinct and individual, not pervasive, making them just the opposite of the previous group of five universally interactive. Each one of these is individually produced from "climbing upon"[1] a certain state, separate from the other four, hence the name "particular state". These five come into being when the "climbing mind" climbs upon an associated state.

As has already been discussed, at the level of the five universally pervasive dharmas, thoughts of good and evil have not yet formed. At that point, one could suppress the mind processes and thereby keep such thoughts from being produced. If one works hard at cultivating, one can keep from

---

[1] "Climbing upon" is *alambana* in Sanskrit and means "support," in this case, for a thought or mental process. The Chinese use of the characters that mean "climb upon" to describe the action of the mind on a dharma comes from this meaning. The mind "climbs upon" dharmas in the same way that other senses respond to their corresponding sense objects. "Climbing upon" refers to the various ways in which the mind sets up factors that make states arise or act as a support for those states.

producing thoughts of good and evil. If one can manage not to produce thoughts of good and evil, then there will not be any creation of good or evil karma. However, if one gives rise to these dharmas of five particular states, among the Dharmas Belonging to the Mind, then one can no longer stop thoughts of good and evil from arising. Therefore, the actual "doing" of good and evil begins with these five particular states.

Of the five particular states, the first one is **desire**. What is meant by desire? It is the wanting of something. Once one wants something, the next thing that happens is that one tries to get it—to grasp at it. That is the result of desire. What does one want to get most? Pleasurable states. One wants to have pleasurable experiences.

Two, **resolution**, is rendered in Chinese by a pair of characters that mean literally "supreme understanding." This mental dharma functions when a state arises that one wants to investigate, to figure out. One becomes involved in the situation, and is determined to figure it out, to understand what it is all about. One becomes quite intent upon this, thinking things like, "What shall I do about it? I've got to come to terms with this and resolve it." One feels one must make up one's mind about it and know exactly what's going on with it. When one is intent upon this process of resolution, if other causes and conditions arise during that time, they will not be able to shake one's mind or prevent it from making this resolution. That is why the Chinese uses "supreme understanding," to try and indicate the intensity behind this dharma of resolution.

Three, **recollection** means "remembering clearly." What does one remember clearly? One remembers the states one has already experienced. For example, an adult may be able to recollect what he studied in grammar school. That is an example of this dharma—clearly remembering and not forgetting—which is the third particular state.

Although the Sanskrit for four, **concentration**, is *samadhi*, what is being described is not *samadhi* as defined in the list of precepts, *samadhi*, and wisdom: the three non-outflow studies. Here we render the word in English as concentration, because it means exclusively paying attention to something. It means to be without distractions in one's mind. It means continually thinking about something or focusing one's attention on it. When this dharma is functioning, your mind will be concentrated on one particular experience to the exclusion of all others. This kind of single-minded concentration is something an ordinary person is capable of. One uses it when performing some activity which one wants to bring to successful accomplishment.

And sometimes, with that much concentration, five, an accuracy of **judgment** will arise, which is the fifth particular state. Although the Sanskrit for this fifth dharma is *prajna*, it is not referring to genuine wisdom, but to an ability which the average person possesses. It is not the *prajna* wisdom which people who cultivate the Way are working to bring forth. Here, we call it judgment, for it refers to being worldly wise, which involves the ability to make judgments and decisions, to have a "sense of judgment." It functions when one tries to figure out if something one did was done well or not, done correctly or incorrectly. That is judgment, worldly wisdom.

When it is a question of wisdom of world-transcending dharmas, *samadhi* and *prajna* help each other out. Samadhi assists *prajna* wisdom, and *prajna* wisdom enhances *samadhi*. That is how *samadhi* and wisdom work on the world-transcending level. But when we speak of the concentration and judgment which are worldly dharmas, they remain isolated from each other. They do not mutually function. It is not the case that if one has concentration then one will have judgment, or that if one has judgment one will have concentration. These worldly dharmas of concentration and judgment cannot happen at the same time. When one is in the midst of concentration, one will not be using the dharma of judgment; and when one is in the process of using judgment, one will not be simultaneously using concentration. Hence, at the mundane level, these two dharmas of concentration and judgment are separate.

All of these five particular states are the same way, isolated from each other. Each one deals with its own particular state. It is not that each one pervades all five, so that one state includes all five states. The previous five universally interactive dharmas were such that one kind of state was replete with five types of minds. These five particular states are isolated from each other, so their states are altogether different. Since they are not the same, let us look at how each arises. Desire arises for pleasurable states. In states requiring decisiveness, resolution is produced. Toward states one has already experienced, one gives rise to recollection. Concentration is initiated toward states that one contemplates, and then judgment arises. Thus we distinguish them from the previous five universally interactive, and call them the five particular states.

Shastra

Three, the eleven wholesome dharmas are:

1. faith;
2. vigor;
3. remorse;
4. shame;
5. absence of greed;
6. absence of anger;
7. absence of foolishness;
8. light ease;
9. non-laxness;
10. renunciation; and,
11. non-harming.

Commentary

This is the third of six divisions of the Fifty-one Dharmas Belonging to the Mind. These **eleven wholesome dharmas are** good dharmas, and so are called wholesome. They help you to cultivate and accomplish your work.

Of the eleven wholesome dharmas, the first is **faith**. Faith is necessary in whatever one does. One needs to have a sense of confidence, an attitude of belief. First one needs to have faith in oneself. What kind of faith? One needs to have faith that one certainly can become a Buddha. One has to believe that there is no difference between the Buddha and oneself. But that non-differentiation is in the Buddha-nature. In order to actually become a Buddha, cultivation is still required. If one cultivates, one will become a Buddha. In order to do so, one must have an initial belief in that principle.

Second, not only does one want to believe that one can become a Buddha oneself, but also to believe that all people can become Buddhas. However, not only can all people become Buddhas, one should believe that all living beings have the Buddha-nature and are capable of becoming Buddhas. If one has that kind of faith, then one should begin by following the rules oneself. To follow the rules means to hold the precepts. First, one holds the precepts, and then one can become a Buddha. One does that oneself, and also encourages others, all living beings, to do so as well. Faith must be solid, like a rock, firm and sturdy. Faith should not be like a pile of ashes that seems to have some substance to it, but crumbles at the slightest disturbance. Do not be too soft. One's faith must be strong and solid.

Once one has solid faith, then one should put it into action with the second wholesome dharma, **vigor**. What should one be vigorous doing? One should be vigorous in cultivating. Be mindful of the Buddha, mindful of the Dharma, and mindful of the Sangha. Use vigor in doing that. Do not always be retreating. One should always keep advancing, being more and more vigorous.

Three is **remorse**, which also carries the meaning of repentance. This dharma is enacted with regard to one's self. One should bring forth an attitude of remorse and repentance, thinking, "The things I have done are really not right. I ought to change and become a new person."

Number four is **shame**. This dharma of shame is enacted with regard to others. One should harbor a sense of shame akin to embarrassment, thinking, "I'm not up to that person. I should not feel that I am better than other people. That person is actually much better than I am. See how that person is always in such good spirits and free from worry? Why is it that I have so many worries?" That is the kind of attitude one should have.

Five is **absence of greed**. Do not be greedy. The way greed works is that if there is something one has not gotten, then one wants to get it. But after getting it, one fears losing it. Both the desire to obtain and the fear of losing are aspects of greed. Therefore, do not be greedy for wealth, do not be greedy for beautiful forms, do not be greedy for fame, and do not be greedy for profit.

I teach you not to be greedy, but I, myself, must be greedy. However, I am being greedy on your behalf. I am greedy for everyone else's sake, not for my own sake. The greed that I have exists on behalf of all cultivators in America. What is it I am greedy for? I am greedy for a Way-place for you Americans to cultivate in. If you all have a Way-place together, you can cultivate the Way. If you do not even have a Way-place, how can you cultivate the Way? To have the Way, you must have a place. And so, I have become greedy for a Way-place, and now it is about to appear as a response to my greed. To begin with, I was not going to become greedy; but I see that if I am not, your opportunities for becoming Buddhas will evolve a lot more slowly. That is the motivation behind my greed, that all of you can become Buddhas a little sooner. All of you should help me out with this greed of mine. I just told you not to be greedy, and now I am telling you to be greedy! But this kind of greed is for the sake of others, not for oneself, so do not hesitate to have more of this kind of greed.

Greed, anger, and foolishness are known as the three poisons, and absence of greed, absence of anger, and absence of foolishness are called the three kinds of good roots.

⊞ The Three Poisons ⊞

1. Greed.
2. Anger.
3. Foolishness.

⊞ The Three Kinds of Good Roots ⊞

1. Absence of greed.
2. Absence of anger.
3. Absence of foolishness.

We are told not to be greedy. If one is greedy for oneself, one is indeed greedy; but if one is greedy for the sake of living beings, one is not actually being greedy. However, a certain fault can develop out of this. It is very easy for people to become hypocritical, rationalizing that what they want is for the sake of all beings, when in fact they want it for their own sakes. People who have this fault can be very clever at instigating what they want in a way that others fail to recognize their real motives. But, as long as one has a personal stake in it, there is still greed.

What, then, is meant by not having a personal stake in it? If one is not seeking fame for oneself; if one is not seeking profit for oneself; if one is not seeking any kind of self-benefit at all, then one does not have a personal stake in it.

Why is greed considered unwholesome? Because it is a defiled kind of dharma. It is unclean. Anyone who is greedy, therefore, is also unclean. One has defilement and filth, and one has attachments. That is why greed is not good. Retributions involving suffering come as a result of having been greedy in the past. Any suffering due you in the future, would be the result of present greed.

Six is **absence of anger**. Do not be angry, either. Anger is a kind of hostility harbored within.

Seven is **absence of foolishness** and is characterized by murkiness. It is ignorance, a lack of clarity.

Absence of greed, absence of anger, and absence of foolishness become the Three Kinds of Good Roots.

Eight, **light ease**, is an initial expedient in the cultivation of Chan *samadhi*. In the process of cultivation, before *samadhi* is actually achieved, one experiences a kind of light ease. Where does this state come from? It comes from being vigorous in cultivating wholesome dharmas and in stopping evil dharmas. Along with being vigorous in wholesome dharmas, one must vigorously abstain from greed, abstain from anger, and abstain from foolishness, practicing the three kinds of good roots discussed above. The resultant merit and virtue will manifest as a state of light ease, an incredibly comfortable feeling of both body and mind. Then, whenever one sits in meditation investigating Chan, one experiences an unsurpassed happiness, an extremely blissful state. That is what is meant here by light ease.

Nine is **non-laxness**. Not being lax means adhering the rules. When one is not lax, one adheres to the rules and relies on the Dharma to cultivate. To never be casual or aloof at any time is what is meant by not being lax.

And what is an example of being lax? During the first summer session (1968), when listening to lectures, one of my disciples used to take his legs out of full lotus, stretch them out full length and prop them on a cushion in front of him. That is an example of being lax. However, he does not do that anymore, which is an example of non-laxness.

Ten, **renunciation**, specifically refers to renouncing everything within the activities *skandha*. One renounces whatever is not in accord with the rules. The renunciation one does with regard to the activities *skandha* is different from the renunciation that takes place with regard to the feeling *skandha*. Renunciations within the feeling *skandha* are made as soon as one has an awakening to them. But renunciation within the activities *skandha* is not so obvious. We know that the activities *skandha* involves a ceaseless flow of thoughts. Within this, one must renounce everything that arises which is not in accord with the rules. For every little bit that is renounced, one comes that much closer to a response with the Way. If in every thought one is capable of this kind of renunciation, then in every thought one enters the Way.

Eleven is **non-harming**. This means not harming any living being. Absence of anger is different from non-harming. Absence of anger involves not reciprocating when someone else directs anger at one, or shows hostility towards one, or does not do what one wants him or her to do. It is a passive stance. But non-harming is a restraint on one's own aggressive tendencies. It refers to how one treats others, specifically by not harming them. Absence of anger means not retaliating when confronted with opposition, whereas non-harming means not initiating any kind of harm toward others.

Four, the six fundamental afflictions
are:

1. greed;
2. anger;
3. foolishness;
4. arrogance;
5. doubt; and,
6. improper views.

Commentary

Division **four** is **the six fundamental afflictions**, which in turn bring about the subsidiary or derivative afflictions. The six fundamental afflictions are actually the Five Dull Servants: **greed, anger, foolishness, arrogance** and **doubt**, together with the Five Sharp Servants, or **improper views**: the view of a body, extreme views, the view of grasping at prohibitions, the view of grasping at views, and deviant views.

⊞ The Five Dull Servants ⊞

1. Greed.
2. Anger.
3. Foolishness.
4. Arrogance.
5. Doubt.

⊞ The Five Sharp Servants ⊞

1. View of a body.
2. Extreme views.
3. View of grasping at prohibitions.

4. View of grasping at views.
5. Deviant views.

Greed, anger, foolishness, arrogance and doubt are called the five dull servants, because they entail a lack of understanding, an inability to make sound judgments. Furthermore, their onset is very slow and obtuse: hence the name, "dull servants." The sharp ones, on the other hand, are very quick, able to assess situations quite rapidly and decisively.

The first one of these afflictions is greed. Greed is impossible to satisfy. There is greed for wealth, for sex, for fame, for food, and for sleep, as well as greed for forms, sounds, smells, tastes, and objects of touch.

Second is anger. Being greedy and then not obtaining the object of one's greed leads to the arising of anger. When things do not go according to one's wishes, one becomes angry. Once anger arises, it culminates in foolish behavior. Foolishness, the third, is just ignorance, a lack of clarity, a confusion that causes one to do muddled and inappropriate things. In this frame of mind, one might do anything.

The fourth is arrogance. Being arrogant, proud, and haughty, one looks down on everyone else and has a very contemptuous attitude.

Five is doubt. Being doubtful, when something comes up, one cannot make up one's mind about it, is never quite sure about it, and never knows quite what to think.

Six is improper views. As mentioned, this single fundamental affliction divides into five parts.

1. The view of a body. One is attached to one's own body as being "me" or "mine." One regards the body as belonging to and comprising oneself and regards what belongs to a self as actually being oneself.

2. Extreme views. The view of a body leads to extreme views, and then causing one to be prejudiced to one extreme or another. If one does not lean too far to the left, then one leans too far to the right. If one does not go too far, one does not go far enough. One is not in accord with the Middle Way, hence the term "extreme views".

3. The view of grasping at views. This kind of grasping is the same grasping found in the Twelve-fold Conditioned Arising. This is the deviant view of mistaking what is not a result for a result. People with this kind of view may claim to have attained an unattainable result.

4. The view of grasping at prohibitions. This is the observance of precepts that should not be observed. For instance, in India there are those who adopt the behavior of cows and dogs as precepts. A person with

this kind of view mistakes what was not a legitimate cause for a legitimate cause.

5. Deviant views. People with deviant knowledge and deviant views would not speak proper Dharma. However, they would willingly talk about defiled dharmas. This means particularly discussing the affairs between men and women, saying what men are like and what women are like. That is to be steeped in deviant views, leading them to say things like, "You do not need to hold the precepts; only stupid people hold precepts. People with wisdom do not need to hold them." They continue talking about defiled dharmas, until eventually their listeners, who originally did not harbor thoughts of desire or have defiled thinking, are caused to give rise to them. Someone may be very pure and clear of mind and just on the verge of obtaining the state of Chan *samadhi*, having gotten rid of the "guest-dust." But, encountering someone who discusses defiled things, that person lets the "guest-dust" back in again, and starts having thoughts of desire.

And so, when you lecture on the Dharma, whether you are a monastic or a layperson, a man or woman, you should not discuss defiled dharmas. You should speak on the Dharmas of purity. You should purify the six sense faculties, and not cause people to have thoughts of desire. If you do speak about defiled dharmas, in the future you are sure to undergo a most terrible retribution.

Thus far we have discussed the eleven wholesome dharmas, followed by the six fundamental afflictions. Next, we will discuss the twenty derivative afflictions, which arise in the wake of the six fundamental afflictions.

Five, the twenty derivative afflictions
are:

1. wrath;
2. hatred;
3. rage;
4. covering;
5. deceit;
6. flattery;
7. conceit;
8. harming;
9. jealousy;
10. stinginess;
11. lack of remorse;
12. lack of shame;
13. lack of faith;
14. laziness;
15. laxness;
16. torpor;
17. restlessness;
18. distraction;

19. improper
    knowledge; and,
20. scatteredness.

Commentary

Division five is the twenty derivative afflictions, called "derivative," because they result from the six fundamental afflictions.

⊞ **The Three Grades of Derivative Afflictions** ⊞

1. Major-grade derivative afflictions
2. Intermediate-grade derivative afflictions
3. Minor-grade derivative afflictions

⊞ **The Three Groups of Derivative Afflictions** ⊞

1. Typical intermediate-grade afflictions
2. Typical major-grade afflictions
3. Typical minor-grade afflictions

These groupings are illustrated by the saying:

> People of the same type gather together.
> Things are classed in similar groups.

For instance, people who study the Buddhadharma gather together in one place. People who study demonic dharmas go to places where demonic dharmas are taught. People who want to learn mundane dharmas find a place where mundane dharmas can be studied. Things, too, are divided into separate groups according to their type. Their varieties and distinctions are inexpressibly many.

⊞ **The Three Factors Involving Derivative Afflictions** ⊟

1. Reinforcement by types.
2. Pervasive infection by the unwholesome nature.
3. Permeation by two defilements of the mind.
   a. Defilement by covering.
   b. Indeterminate defilement.

· · ·

1. Reinforcement by types. This is when intermediate-grade afflictions are produced together with other intermediate-grade afflictions, major-grade afflictions are produced together with other major-grade afflictions, and minor-grade afflictions are produced together with other minor-grade afflictions.

2. Pervasive infection by the unwholesome nature. Pervasive infection means that the afflictions interact and influence each other. For instance, lack of remorse

also brings about lack of shame, because if one is not repentant, one will also not feel ashamed. Another example is lack of faith, which gives rise in turn to laziness, laxness, and other derivative afflictions.

3. Permeation by two defilements of the mind.
    a. Defilement by covering.

Covering means keeping things hidden and not allowing anyone to know.

    b. Indeterminate defilement.

Indeterminate means the defilement cannot be categorized as to its relative goodness or evil. If all three factors are present, the affliction is a major grade one. If two factors are present, the affliction is an intermediate grade one. If none of the three factors is present, then the affliction that has arisen is an isolated one and is thus classified as a minor-grade affliction.

First, we will discuss the ten minor derivative afflictions. Number one is **wrath**. Wrath occurs when a state arises which is in opposition to one's wishes. When something is not going one's way, when something is really bothering one, when one becomes very emotional about something, then wrath can arise. It comes on suddenly and is a combination of anger and hatred, an unexpected and intense emotional reaction.

Two is **hatred**. This affliction occurs when one is faced with situations similar to the ones described above, but one does not vent one's wrath. Instead, one represses the emotional feelings deep inside. The hatred which results then becomes like a rope, binding one's heart in a tight knot.

Three is **rage**. The Chinese character for rage also occurs in the pair of Chinese characters that means affliction. This emotional reaction is much more severe than hatred. When rage happens, one literally explodes. When things become unbearable, one gets infuriated. Rage is a very fierce emotional reaction.

Four is **covering**. This is hiding something inside, keeping it bottled up and not allowing it to surface. Basically, one is quite afflicted about something, feeling the kinds of wrath, hatred, and rage described above, but fears the reactions of the other person. And so one keeps the emotions to oneself and is not straightforward about expressing those feelings. One does not say, "I can't stand you," "I'm not happy with you," or anything of the sort. One conceals and represses one's feelings, storing them up inside and not revealing them to the person directly. Then, when the time comes, one assassinates the person. Openly one might not succeed in harming him, so one stabs him in the back to do him in.

Five is **deceit**. Deceit is a false kindness and phony intention. One appears to be kindly but in fact is not really that way. For instance, one may say, "I have some dope here which I'll give you free. Here, take some." The person takes the drugs and thereupon becomes addicted. Having an addiction, he is then forced to buy dope from the one who "gave" him the stuff "free" to begin with. That is an example of deceit.

Six is **flattery**. This means playing up to people, being obsequious. It means being a sycophant, puffing people up, giving them high hats to wear. For instance one says, "Oh, Sir, where are you going. I was thinking of going to see you. I have a friend who really thinks highly of you. He is going to want to get together with you and include you in a big business deal he has going," and so forth.

Flattery means playing up to those who are rich when one is poor. Just because someone is wealthy, one addresses that person with all kinds of deference, using venerable titles and polite phrases. "You're quite a fellow, a truly great man. You are a distinguished person. You're really wonderful." This occurs when ordinary people are before the President. They scramble for words, searching for all the nicest things to say and falling all over themselves to make an impression in expressing them.

Seven is **conceit**. One caught up in this affliction has a disproportionate sense of one's own worth. Basically, one does not have much sense, but one thinks more highly of oneself then one does of others. For example, one may be uneducated and yet say things like, "What do people with education know anyway? What good does it do them? I've never studied, but look at me. There's good food on my table and I've got plenty of money in my pocket." That is being conceited. One feels one's own value surpasses that of other people.

Eight is **harming**. With this affliction one wants to harm others. One of the eleven wholesome dharmas was non-harming. This affliction is the exact opposite of the good dharma.

Nine is **jealousy.** This affliction occurs when one becomes envious of those who surpass one in some way or other. For example, someone may be endowed with an excellent memory. Because of this, one becomes jealous of that person thinking, "If only that person weren't around, then I would be number One. As long as he's here I don't get to be First." That is jealousy. Or one may get jealous of someone with a higher level of education than one possesses, and end up thinking the same kind of thought: "As long as that person is around, I can't be Number One. Without that person, I would be the most highly educated one here." Being jealous of anyone who surpasses one in any way is included in the definition of this affliction.

Ten is **stinginess**. With this affliction, one is tight with one's benefits, not wishing to share them with others. One is unable to give anything away. For instance, if a stingy person has money and it is suggested he part with some of it, he simply cannot bring himself to do so. He hangs on to that money, squeezing every penny of it so tightly that it turns to liquid and melts away in his palm. Then he wonders where it went. The pigeons were no doubt stingy in past lives in addition to being greedy. They could not give up their possessions so now they must endure the retribution of always having to "sponge" off others. They do not have anything of their own. If you suggested to a pigeon that it give anything away, it would not be able to do it. Those are the ten minor-grade derivative afflictions. Next are the two intermediate-grade derivative afflictions.

Eleven is **lack of remorse**. One of the eleven wholesome dharmas is remorse, and so this affliction is its opposite. One who lacks remorse always feels self-righteous. One assumes one is entitled to do whatever one wishes. One considers oneself a special person, an exceptional individual. Those who call themselves extraordinary simply have no sense of remorse. They lack a feeling of repentance.

Twelve is **lack of shame**. One who lacks shame never really examines whether or not one is up to the standards of others. One never feels that what one does might not be on a par with what others do, nor does one fear ridicule or reprisal. One has no concern for public opinion and feels no sense of embarrassment even when the things one does are in fact mean and lowly. Such a person lacks the feeling of shame. Last, we will look at the eight major-grade derivative afflictions.

Thirteen is **lack of faith**. Among the eleven wholesome dharmas was faith. This affliction is the exact opposite. One does not believe in anyone. One does not trust one's teacher or anyone else. If the teacher lacks faith, he does not trust his disciples. If the disciples lack faith, they do not trust the teacher. A son who lacks faith will not trust even his father, and a father who lacks faith will not believe his son, much less need we mention siblings. Brothers and sisters who lack faith will not believe in each other. Their attitude will be, "How can you expect me to trust you? You should believe in me."

When one gets to the point of thinking that others should believe in one, always convinced that one is quite great, then no matter what others tell one, one will doubt its validity. If one speaks the Dharma for a person who lacks faith, the reaction will be, "That's just a bunch of phony words; it's all false. You call that Dharma? What kind of Dharma, anyway? You're just trying to trick us." That is the attitude of one who lacks faith. But actually that is not so far off, for when I speak the Dharma, there is not a single bit of truth in it. You should not listen to it. In fact, you should run away really fast. An example is the person outside the door who stated clearly, "I'm an outsider," and upon being asked to come in, ran away. That is lack of faith.

Fourteen is **laziness**. This affliction is the exact opposite of vigor. It is being actively non-vigorous. It is another name for indolence.

Fifteen is **laxness**. Another of the eleven wholesome dharmas was non-laxness. This affliction is its opposite. It means one does not follow the rules but does whatever one pleases. It is akin to the "freedom" or "independence" that Americans advocate. When that concept is carried too far it results in laxness. Laxness means not obeying one's parents, but proceeding to do exactly what one wants. This particular affliction is a major reason why it is such a headache teaching Americans. You laugh, but it is true.

Sixteen is **torpor**. This is the affliction of wanting to nod off during the *sutra* lectures. In fact, it does not matter what one is doing, with this affliction, one wants to fall asleep in the process. Reading a *sutra*, one wants to fall asleep. Bowing to the Buddhas, one wants to nod off. While translating *sutras*, one has the urge to sleep. Listening to the *sutra* lectures, one is even less willing to stay awake. Torpor is another name for sleepiness. However, torpor is different from foolishness. Foolishness is a general darkness and lack of clarity, an inability to understand what is going on. Torpor is a dream-like, foggy state of mind in which one is oblivious to what is going on around one. One is sitting there, and suddenly everything goes blank. One cannot remember anything that has been happening. Listening to *sutras*, one suddenly can not remember anything that was just said. It is like being in a dream and yet is not actually dreaming. It is what is described in the verse:

> If one who is deluded transmits it to another,
> After all is said and done, neither one understands.
> The teacher falls into the hells,
> And the disciple burrows in after him.

Seventeen is **restlessness**. With this affliction, one is agitated and cannot keep still, like the demon-king who came here the other day. One is unable to manage the cultivation of calm, pure states. One runs around aimlessly and chaotically. Sitting, one gets restless and decides to stand. Standing, one gets agitated and decides to sit. Walking, one starts out going north and ends up headed south or starts out east and ends up going west. One is all over the place, unable to settle down. That is what happens to the body.

One's mouth is just as chaotic. Saying whatever one pleases, one "runs off at the mouth" like that demon-king that day, full of chaotic and confusing talk.

Restlessness also affects the mind. One does a tremendous amount of uncontrolled thinking. One thought replaces the next in an aimless wandering that goes off on tangents and cannot stick to the point. One starts out thinking about one thing, and ends up thinking about something entirely different. One's thinking enters "Never-never Land" and starts to fantasize wildly. "I ascended to the heavens where a god told me that in three days I'd get reborn in the heavens. Now did that really happen?" One thinks about things one has no business thinking about. "I went to a certain place in meditation and ended up suspended in empty space. Did that really happen? Or will it happen?" The mind becomes tangled in chaos as one contrives all kinds of non-existent experiences. See how pathetic this Restlessness is?

Eighteen is **distraction**. With this affliction one loses proper mindfulness, and is only mindful of the deviant. It is another way to enter "Fantasy Land." But in this case one ends up thinking about things that are not wholesome. Whatever goes against the rules, this person thinks about. But what accords with the rules, he does not think about. His thinking does not accord with the rules when he indulges in this affliction.

Nineteen is **improper knowledge**. With this affliction, one becomes obsessed with defilement. It is all one knows. There is nothing proper at all in one's knowledge.

And twenty is **scatteredness**. Scatteredness entails totally wild confusion. The mind becomes mixed-up and divided against itself. This affliction is different from restlessness.

If we were to go into the subtle details of each one, a lot could be said. This will suffice to introduce these twenty derivative afflictions to you. Now that you know about them, I hope that you will give rise to more afflictions, to the point that you will eat your fill of afflictions, and not have to eat food. Then, if there were a famine, you would not die of hunger, because you would have lots of afflictions to eat.

Six, the four unfixed are:

1. sleep;
2. regret;
3. investigation; and,
4. examination.

Commentary

The Fifty-one Dharmas Belonging to the Mind are grouped into six divisions, of which we have already discussed five. Now we come to division **six, the four unfixed**. They **are** known as unfixed because they are basically indeterminate. Since there is nothing fixed about them, they are called unfixed. If there were anything definite about them, they would not be said to be "unfixed." They are indeterminate in that they are not necessarily wholesome dharmas, and not necessarily defiled dharmas. A decidedly wholesome dharma would be, for example, bringing forth the Bodhi resolve. A decidedly defiled dharma would be bringing forth thoughts of lust. Another way these dharmas are unfixed is that they do not necessarily pervade all minds and do not necessarily pervade all grounds. How many unfixed dharmas are there? There are four kinds.

The first one is **sleep** in the text we are using, although most texts have what is here two, **regret**, listed first. Sleep is a kind of dark obscurity, a blackness and lack of clarity. But the lack of clarity does not mean inability to understand. Rather, it refers to a darkness that pervades all you do. Sleep can result in two problems. Externally, it deprives you of affinities with other people, and internally it blocks contemplation.

Hence sleep can lead to social isolation, and can cause you to lack wisdom. This dark lack of clarity is an unfixed dharma.

The second one, regret, is sometimes called self reproach. What does one regret? When these dharmas are being explained, you should pay close attention. Be very attentive and do not let the explanation of them pass by your ears like a breeze, so that although I explain so many dharmas for you, afterwards you still do not understand. When it is time to lose your temper, you still lose your temper. When it comes time to get angry, you go ahead and get angry just the same, and are not the least bit able to apply what you have learned. As soon as you hear it, it evaporates. If that is the case, then there has been no use at all in listening to this explanation. If you listen to the Sutras with that attitude, then even a hundred great eons of doing so would not be of any great use.

It should be that, having heard a lecture you think, "The Shastra is telling me I shouldn't have afflictions, so from now on I'm not going to have even one of the twenty derivative afflictions, and will basically not let the six fundamental afflictions arise." That is the way someone who has brought forth the resolve for Bodhi applies them. It should not be that as the afflictions are being explained, and the more names for them you learn, the more of them you give rise to. That is what I was talking about when I advised you before that you could now "eat" more afflictions. Previously you did not know, but now when you get angry you can wonder whether you should be using wrath or hatred. Before, you did not understand there were so many afflictions to choose from, and now that you know, it has greatly expanded your repertoire. You think, "Let's see, now is a good time to use rage; or maybe covering is in order. That way I can destroy you behind your back." If that is what you are learning, then you are making a big mistake. You have listened to the Shastra in vain.

Regret is also sometimes listed as self-reproach, because it arises with regard to deeds not done right. "Why did I do that, anyway?" Having done something wrong, one regrets it. Or one regrets not having done some bad things to someone, thinking things like, "Why didn't I do such-and-such a thing to that particular person? That would have put him in his place for sure. It would have totally done him in. Why didn't I think of it then!" Or, "Why didn't I hack off his arm with my knife when I had the chance? That way he couldn't have hit me." It is that kind of regret that is meant here. Regret arises when one is not satisfied with one's actions or inactions, or when one feels one has done something the wrong way. That is the first, regret or self-reproach.

Three is **investigation**, and four is **examination**. Investigation is a coarser dharma than examination. When you are just about to act in a way that could be good or bad, you do a kind of reckoning with yourself. You hold a meeting with yourself in your mind, and take stock of what you are about to do. You think to yourself, "If I handle this matter in such-and-such a way, will it turn out well?" Then you answer yourself, "No! Don't do that! How could you?" In this way you have a meeting with yourself. If this meeting in your mind is on a coarse level, then it is called investigation. This is when you obviously are going back and forth with yourself.

But if your thinking is very subtle, then it is called examination. These two unfixed Dharmas Belonging to the Mind have discursive thought as their basis and result in a kind of discrimination. Investigation and examination are like that. We have now completed discussion of the sixth division; namely, the four unfixed Dharmas Belonging to the Mind.

The third is the Form Dharmas. In general, there are eleven kinds:

1. eyes;
2. ears;
3. nose;
4. tongue;
5. body;
6. forms;
7. sounds;
8. smells;
9. flavors;
10. objects of touch; and,
11. dharmas pertaining to form.

Commentary

To review, so far we have discussed the first overall category of Eight Mind Dharmas, and the second overall category of Fifty-one Dharmas Belonging to the Mind. Now we come to **the third** major group, which is **the Form Dharmas**. Form Dharmas are those which have shape and substantial physical form, a kind of obstructive quality. They have substantial shape that can be seen, and obstructiveness that can be interacted with. They stand in contrast to the Mind Dharmas and Dharmas Belonging to the Mind.

Number one is **eyes**. The eyes are classified as a form dharma, because not only can they see all kinds of forms, they are themselves physical forms. They have a substantial shape and can be seen. When the eyes see things that are enjoyable to look at, they never get tired of looking at them. But if they look at things which are unpleasant to see, they object to the sight and resist looking.

Two is **ears**. The ears hear all kinds of sounds. If the ears hear sounds that are pleasurable, they can listen day after day without any sense of fatigue. But as soon as they hear something that is not pleasant, they do not like it and quickly grow tired of it.

Three is **nose**. The nose smells scents, and if they are pleasant and fragrant, then the more it smells the better it likes it. It never grows tired of smelling. But if it has to smell some stench, it will object from the moment it gets a whiff of it and grow tired of it immediately.

Four is **tongue**. The tongue tastes flavors. If they are pleasant flavors, the tongue is delighted to taste them. If the flavors are unpleasant, it does not like to taste them. It says, "Ugh, that's too bitter! I don't want to eat it!"

Five is **body**. If the body likes something, it wants to get near it and come into contact with it. If it does not like something, it wants to stay far away from it. Those five Form Dharmas just discussed are the five internal sense organs. The sixth in the list, the faculty of the mind, is not a form dharma, because the intellect belongs to the sixth consciousness, making it a mind dharma.

Six, **forms**; seven, **sounds**; eight, **smells**; nine, **flavors**; and ten, **objects of touch** are all included under the category of Form Dharmas. They are the five external sense objects, or dusts.

Number eleven of the Form Dharmas is **dharmas pertaining to form**. This is classed as a type of form dharma, because these dharmas are the shadows cast within the intellect by the five external dusts. Thus, even though they happen in the mind, they belong to form. What is the origin of these Eleven Form Dharmas? It is the Nature of the Treasury of the Thus Come One. All these dharmas are composed of the four elements.

⊞ The Four Elements ⊞

1. Earth.
2. Water.
3. Fire.
4. Air.

Eyes, ears, nose, tongue, body, forms, sounds, smells, flavors, objects of touch, and dharmas pertaining to form are composed of the four elements. These sense organs and the sense objects are formed by the coming together of the four elements.

Besides that, earth, air, fire, and water fill the entire Dharma Realm. In the *Shurangama Sutra*, the principle of the four elements is discussed in detail, and it is shown how they are all the nature of the Treasury of the Thus Come One. We ordinary we people consider fire and water to be incompatible. However, water pervades the entire Dharma Realm, as does fire. Air and earth also entirely pervade the Dharma Realm. Within the Dharma Realm they assist one another and do not interfere with one another. Water is not incompatible with fire and fire does not hinder water. They all get along just fine! How can this be? It is because in nature they are all the Treasury of the Thus Come One. Our bodies start out as being the four elements, and from these arise all the various dharmas. People who have never listened to the *sutras* before may find it hard to fathom how our bodies are composed of the four elements, but if you look into it in detail, it will become clear to you, and you will know that it is true.

Take for example the moist parts of your body, the perspiration, urine, and all the other liquids. These belong to the element water. Your temperature belongs to the element fire. Your breath belongs to the element air. And your skin, flesh, muscles, and bones belong to the element earth. When the four elements come together in this way, then the Eleven Form Dharmas result. This has been just a brief explanation of how these Form Dharmas come about. If you really want to know about them, you will have to become enlightened, and then you will be able to completely fathom them.

There are only two major categories of dharmas left, and so my explanation of them will soon be completed. Then, the question of whether or not you enter this "door to understanding" lies with you. Whether I have explained them clearly is my concern. Whether you have listened to them clearly is your concern. If you are clear, then you will understand these hundred dharmas. If you are not clear, then you will not have understood them. If you understand these hundred dharmas, then you will be able to understand all the essential principles of Buddhism. If you have understood them, then it can be said you have opened an enlightenment. If you have not understood them, you can keep studying them gradually.

The fourth is Activities Dharmas Non-interactive with the Mind. In general, there are twenty-four:

1. attainment;
2. life-faculty;
3. generic similarity;
4. dissimilarity;
5. the No-thought Samadhi;
6. the Samadhi of Extinction;
7. the Reward of No-Thought;
8. bodies of nouns;
9. bodies of sentences;
10. bodies of phonemes;
11. birth;
12. dwelling;

Shastra

13. aging;
14. impermanence;
15. revolving;
16. distinction;
17. interaction;
18. speed;
19. sequence;
20. time;
21. direction;
22. numeration;
23. combination; and,
24. discontinuity.

Commentary

The fourth is the Activities Dharmas Non-interactive with the Mind. Non-interactive explained in contemporary terms means not cooperating. You do not cooperate with me, and I do not cooperate with you. For example, if I say, "Let's go east," and you insist on going west, then that is not cooperating, and we are non-interactive. If we are interactive, then we cooperate. In that case, when I say "to the east," you also go east, and when I suggest heading west, you go west, too. Another example of interaction is when we take some grain in our hands and the pigeons come and eat out of our hands. We have the grain and they want to eat it, so we interact. But if they did not eat it, then there would not be any interaction.

What is it that these **twenty-four** Non-interactive Dharmas do not interact with? They do not interact with the Mind Dharmas. They do not interact with the Dharmas Belonging to the Mind. They do not interact with the Form Dharmas, and even less would they interact with the Unconditioned Dharmas. That is because they are very special.

How is it that they do not interact with the Mind Dharmas or Dharmas Belonging to the Mind? Mind Dharmas and Dharmas Belonging to the Mind are able to "climb on" external states. They have that ability. But these twenty-four non-interactive dharmas do not have the same ability as Mind Dharmas and Dharmas Belonging to the Mind. They are not able to "climb upon" states. Therefore, they are not interactive with Mind Dharmas or Dharmas Belonging to the Mind.

You might say that if they do not interact with Mind Dharmas and Dharmas Belonging to the Mind, at least they should be interactive with Form Dharmas. But they are not interactive with those either. Why not? These dharmas cannot be called Form Dharmas, because they do not have any substance, and they do not have any marks. They have no physical characteristics. All twenty-four of these dharmas are false. They are absolutely and totally false, so do not mistake them for something real. The reason they do not interact with the other dharmas is that they are false and therefore cannot combine with anything else at all. Nonetheless they do exist. But although they exist, they have no substance of their own, no characteristics of their own. Therefore, they do not interact.

They do not have any real shape or characteristics, and so they are false.

You are listening to the Dharma, and there are both true dharmas and false dharmas. Now I am speaking false dharmas for you, but that is because it is necessary for you to know the false dharmas in order for your true nature can appear. If you do not know the false dharmas, how can you attain your true nature? If you mistake the false for the true, then that becomes the false within the false, unreality within unreality. It is false to start with, and you add some further unreality. That is to be like the Venerable Ananda. We cannot simply call him "Ananda," but should add the title "Venerable." He wanted to attain the true, but was afraid of losing the false. He could not give up the false. If you cannot let go of what is false, the true will not manifest. Hence there is the saying:

> If you cannot give up the false,
> You will not accomplish the true.
> If you cannot give up death,
> You cannot exchange it for life.

Now I am telling you about these twenty-four kinds of false dharmas. Although they have no shape or characteristics, they are still subject to production and extinction. Since they are subject to production and extinction, they also are not interactive with the Unconditioned Dharmas. The unconditioned is not subject to production or extinction, but these twenty-four false dharmas all have a nature subject to production and extinction. They are basically shadows cast by the interaction of Form Dharmas, Mind Dharmas, and Dharmas Belonging to the Mind. Consequently, they are false; there is actually nothing true about them.

Someone is thinking, "Today I really wanted to hear some true Dharma, but all this Dharma Master has talked about is false dharmas. If I had known his whole lecture was going to be about false dharmas, I wouldn't have come to listen." Well, if you refuse to hear about false dharmas, then there is no true Dharma. First you have to learn about false dharmas, and then you will be able to recognize true Dharma. Therefore, this is still a case of speaking the false for the sake of the true, and then the false is dispersed so the true appears.

As to these Activities Dharmas Non-interactive with the Mind, in general there are twenty-four. The first one is **attainment**. Attainment means starting out not having something and then getting it. And where does attainment generated from? It arises from greed. Within a state of not wanting anything, you suddenly want to gain something.

For example, you might say, "I've attained a piece of gold. Tell me, is this gold or not?" However, the gold itself is not the attainment. Attainment is a pseudonym, an unreal designation, hence it is a false dharma.

The **life-faculty**, or root of life, comes from seeds residing in the eighth consciousness. When these seeds are vivified, there is life. As soon as the eighth consciousness resides in your body, your body is alive. When the eighth consciousness is in your body, the life faculty is there. When the eighth consciousness leaves your body, life goes with it. Therefore, the root of life, the life faculty, is false as well. Do not think, "This life of mine is true. No matter what, I'm going to take care of this precious body of mine. Nobody can get away with bumping into me. I will not allow anyone to say anything the least bit impolite to me." It is just because you are unable to give up your root of life that you are unable to become enlightened and cannot achieve Buddhahood. The life faculty is actually harmful to you, it is a detriment, but you do not realize it. You think it is a precious treasure. You consider your life to be valuable and important. But that is just an attachment. You are mistaking the false for the true. Your self-nature is true but your life is not true. The life faculty is false.

Three, **generic similarity,** refers to a group having similar shares. For example, you have a body, which is your share and I have a body which is my share. The fact that every person has a body is thus known as a generic similarity. Ordinary people have a generic similarity with other ordinary people; those of the Two Vehicles have a generic similarity with others of the Two Vehicles. There is a generic similarity among Bodhisattvas. However, within these similarities there are also some dissimilarities, the next dharma.

Dissimilarity. Let us take an example of two people. Because they are both people, they have a generic similarity. But one of these people is impetuous. He just barges right in and starts doing things, with a positive attitude. The other person is cautious and somewhat negative. He hesitates to do anything. Now the impetuous person says of the cautious person, "See that guy? He doesn't do anything at all. Just eats and sleeps. What use is he anyway? I think we should just get rid of people like that."

The cautious person says of the impetuous person, "See that guy? He would do anything, anything at all! It's guys like him who are ruining the world! I think we should simply do away with all such people!" Basically these are two human beings but they want to eliminate each other. They end up being jealous and obstructive of each other, and denouncing each other.

There is another good example of dissimilarities within similarities. Take the armor maker and the sword smith. They share a similar occupation, production of armaments. But they are on opposite ends of the spectrum, because the armor maker is intent upon making a product that will be invincible against swords, lances, spears, arrows, and similar kinds of weapons. His aim is to protect the warrior. The sword smith, on the other hand, tries to devise weapons that will pierce the armor. He aims to make his products so sharp that with a single blow they will rend the strongest armor. Although both products are armaments, one product is for defense and the other is for offense. That is a dissimilarity within similarity.

Another example is found within Buddhism itself. Basically all five divisions of Buddhism are similar in that they are aspects of Buddhism. But when contention arises between members of various schools, then dissimilarity occurs within that similarity. That is why when someone came the other night and asked me what sect I adhered to, I replied, "I don't adhere to any one sect." If you do not align yourself with a particular sect, then there is no way anyone can attack you. But, once people align themselves within particular sects, then those of the Chan division say that the teaching school is no good; and those of the teaching division say that the Chan division is wrong. They all slander each other. That is another example of dissimilarity within a generic similarity.

Another example occurs among "worthies". From time immemorial, the worthies have been getting down on one another. One will say, "Oh, Confucius, he's someone who didn't have any sense at all." Or, another will say, "Mencius? He understood even less. I have a lot more wisdom than either one of them." You see? To begin with, they all had a generic similarity, but when they started slandering one another it ended up creating a dissimilarity, due to their varying propensities and habits. This is just a simple explanation. There would be no way to finish if we discussed this in detail.

Five, the **No-Thought Samadhi**, is cultivated by those of externalist ways. They distance themselves from production and extinction. They forcefully prevent the mind and the Dharmas Belonging to the Mind from working. They bring the operation of the mind and the Dharmas Belonging to the Mind to a stop, so that there is no actual thinking. But this is really a forced situation. It is similar to putting a heavy rock on a clump of crab grass to prevent the grass from growing up. But the roots remain. Those immersed in the No-thought Samadhi are still not free of the seventh consciousness's innate attachment to self.

⊞ The Two Innate Attachments of the Seventh Consciousness ⊞

1. The innate attachment to self.
2. The innate attachment to dharmas.

Six is the **Samadhi of Extinction**. This is also a *samadhi* cultivated by those of externalist ways. Again, it is a case of using a kind of force as a means to arrive at extinction. Here, the sixth consciousness and the Dharmas Belonging to the Mind cease to function, just as in the No-Thought Samadhi described above. That means that one in this *samadhi* does not strike up false thoughts, yet again it is very forced. Since false thinking is forcibly extinguished, this is called the Samadhi of Extinction. However, the seventh consciousness's innate attachment to dharmas has not ceased to function. In the one above it was the innate attachment to self, which is the coarser of the two. Here, the attachment is a bit subtler and is the innate attachment to dharmas. The seventh consciousness and the eighth consciousness still mingle together and one is not yet free of them. So, although this is called a *samadhi*, the Samadhi of Extinction is not a true *samadhi*.

Seven, the **Reward of No-Thought** is different from the No-Thought Samadhi, in that the former is a cause, whereas the latter is a result. The No-Thought Samadhi is a kind of state in which one has not yet relinquished one's body. The Reward of No-Thought is when one has already relinquished one's body and receives this Reward of No-Thought. At that time, one is reborn in the Heaven of No-Thought, in the fourth *dhyana*. Although there is no longer any thought, there remains a very subtle attachment to form, which still exists in the eighth consciousness and which one assumes to be one's life. This refers to an extremely subtle aspect of the marks division of the eighth consciousness. It causes a person to still feel that he has a life. But this life still has an end to it, and when that occurs, the person can still fall.

You may remember the practitioner who cultivated to attain the Heaven of No-Thought? When he sat in meditation, he was continually disturbed by a fish jumping in the water, until one day he got angry. He said, "I'm going to turn into a kingfisher and get you, fish. I'm going to eat you up." When he relinquished his body, he was born in the Heaven of Neither Thought nor No-Thought, obtaining his reward of no-thought. But after his heavenly blessings were used up, he fell and was reborn as a kingfisher. When I tell you that these two pigeons here used to monastics who did not keep the precepts, and that is how they have ended up, you should understand it is the same principle.

Eight is **bodies of nouns**. Nouns are the names of people, places, and things. Every human being is called a person, which is a noun. They also each have their own individual names, which are proper nouns. There is also the distinction of general and specific nouns that applies to material objects. For example, we can call this a burner, or more specifically, an incense burner. We can call that a vase, or more specifically a flower vase. Here we refer to a general noun simply as a noun and a noun compound as a body of nouns.

Nine is **bodies of sentences**. Just as bodies of nouns are used to delineate dharmas, so too, are bodies of sentences used to clarify them.

"All activities are impermanent, characterized by production and extinction" is a sentence. When groups of sentences are used to reveal dharmas, they are called bodies of sentences.

Ten is **bodies of phonemes**. Phonemes are sounds that carry meaning in a given language. In Chinese, each character is monosyllabic. When characters are compounded in a meaningful way, they form a body of phonemes. The Sutras are all bodies of phonemes. All kinds of books, articles, treatises, and so forth, are bodies of phonemes.

Eleven is **birth**, and twelve is **dwelling**. Everything subject to birth will also dwell. People, creatures, and things are all subject to thirteen, which is **aging**, and fourteen, which is **impermanence**. With birth, something comes into being that previously did not exist. Aging refers to the decline and decay of something that still exists. Therefore, aging is also known as "changing." During the stage of dwelling one remains stable, but when aging sets in, things become different. These four refer to the cycle of coming into being, dwelling, decaying, and disappearing.

Fifteen, **revolving**; sixteen, **distinction**; and seventeen, **interaction** also relate to each other. Revolving literally means "turning and flowing," and refers to how we people have from beginningless time until the present been turning on the wheel of rebirth in the six paths. We have been flowing and turning in birth and death for myriads of *kalpas* without rest. This process never stops and so it is called revolving.

Distinction means "determining of differences," and refers, for example, to the distinctions that occur in the process of cause and effect. Whatever kind of cause one plants will reap a corresponding result. But sometimes the same kinds of causes can lead to different effects, and that is known as distinction.

Interaction is the next, dharma number seventeen. Someone is wondering how since these twenty-four are called non-interactive there can be one among them called interaction. That is a good question. It appears to be a contradiction, but actually it is not. Basically, these twenty-four dharmas are non-interactive with the dharmas of the other four general categories. They do not interact with Mind Dharmas; they do not interact with Dharmas Belonging to the Mind; they do not interact with Form Dharmas; and, they do not interact with Unconditioned Dharmas. But this dharma of interaction does interact with the dharmas within its own category, the rest of the Twenty-four Activities Dharmas Non-interactive with the Mind. The interaction is that involved with the cycle of cause and effect. The cause is the beginning of the cycle and the effect is the end outcome. Between the cause and the effect there is the mark of karma, which interacts with both the cause and the effect. So this cycle involves the revolution, the distinction, and the interaction. The interaction which occurs is decisive, just like a shadow that follows a shape. It is never inexact by the least bit.

Eighteen, **speed**, refers to an extremely powerful forward momentum. It is found in the flash of lightning; the velocity of wind; the swiftness of a bird flying through the air; the quickness of a rabbit on the run. These are all outward manifestations of speed.

Nineteen, the dharma of **sequence**, refers to things being in regular succession, whether it is from above to below, from front to back, or to layers, series or gradations. It is the presence of ordering and the absence of chaos or confusion.

Twenty is **time**, is a dharma that is revealed in the marking of intervals, such as years, months, days, hours. The shortest interval of time is a *kshana*. The longest interval of time is limitlessly many *kalpas*. Time, too, is a dharma.

Twenty-one, **direction**, refers to location or placement. We distinguish direction by referring to things as being "in front" or "behind," to the "left" or to the "right," "above" or "below," and so forth in relation to other things.

Twenty-two, **numeration**, refers to numbering systems. This, too, is a dharma.

Twenty-three, **combination**, can be blending and uniting, as when milk is homogenized. Or it may be a fitting together, such as of a jar with its lid.

Twenty-four, **discontinuity**, is the opposite of combination, in that it refers to spontaneity as opposed to causation. Externalists attach to the extreme view of spontaneity, whereas those of the Two Vehicles attach to causation, the coming together of causes and conditions. But the Nature of the Treasury of the Thus Come One is neither causation nor spontaneity, neither combination nor discontinuity.

Those are the twenty-four non-interactive dharmas. They do not belong to Form Dharmas, Mind Dharmas, Dharmas Belonging to the Mind, or Unconditioned Dharmas, and so are termed the twenty-four not interactive.

The fifth is the Unconditioned
Dharmas, of which there are, in
general, six:

1. unconditioned
   empty space.
2. unconditioned
   extinction attained
   by selection.
3. unconditioned
   extinction that is
   unselected.
4. unconditioned
   unmoving
   extinction.
5. unconditioned
   extinction of
   feeling and
   thinking.
6. unconditioned
   True Thusness.

Commentary

The fifth major category **is the Unconditioned Dharmas of which there are, in general, six.** One is **unconditioned empty space.** Empty space is basically unconditioned, and could not be conditioned. There is no way to describe it as conditioned. It is empty, empty space. But here the unconditioned refers to one's ability to contemplate empty space. It means to be able to "illumine and view the five *skandhas* all as empty." Then there is no mark of self, no mark of others, no mark of living beings, and no mark of a lifespan.

You may say, "Well, I cultivate and have a little skill. I always sleep sitting up and never lie down. I only eat one meal a day." But if you are still aware that you sleep sitting up and never lie down, then you still have not reached unconditioned empty space. If you still know that you eat only one meal a day, then you still have not reached unconditioned empty space. If you are aware that you cultivate, then you still have not reached unconditioned empty space. That is because unconditioned empty space means your self-nature is like empty space; your body is like empty space; what you contemplate and cultivate is truly devoid of a mark of self, a mark of others, a mark of living beings, and a mark of a lifespan. When you reach that state, then if someone punched you, it would be as if they were punching empty space. Just think what it would be like to punch empty space. Empty space would not put up any resistance at all. Empty space certainly would not hit back. If you can cultivate to the point of being like empty space, then nothing will be able to bother you, for you would have reached empty space. That is the meaning of unconditioned empty space.

Unconditioned empty space is extremely wonderful. I always tell you this, but you never think it is very interesting, because you hear it every day. What is it? It is just, "Everything's okay." If you could really have it be that "everything's okay," then you would be like empty space, because empty space contains everything within it. Can you think of anything that is not in empty space? And there is nothing that empty space rejects. It never gets upsets with you and says, "You, there, who are part of my empty space. You got it so dirty! How can you have gone to the toilet there and gotten my empty space so dirty?" Empty space does not think that way. Pigeons, too, for their part are always up in empty space flying around, and empty space does not get in their way at all.

If we were to fully discuss unconditioned empty space in detail, there would be too much to say. Basically you should always contemplate empty space and reach the point that you have no mark of self, no mark of others, no mark of living beings, and no mark of a lifespan. Then you will unite with the myriad things.

> Unite your virtue with heaven and earth.
> Unite your light with the sun and moon.

Unite your order with that of the four seasons.
Unite your good and bad luck with the ghosts and spirits.

Were you like that, then however great the virtuous nature of heaven was, your virtuous nature would be just that great. The light of the sun is very bright, but your light would be just as bright as the sun's. The moon is also bright, but your light would be as bright as that of the moon. That is what is meant by "uniting one's light with the sun and moon."

Spring, summer, fall, and winter are the four seasons. If you cultivate so that you become just like empty space, then when springtime comes, you have the representation of spring within yourself. In the same way, you represent all the four seasons as they occur. In the spring the myriad things come into being. In the summer the myriad things increase and grow. In the fall the myriad things are harvested, and in the winter they are stored away. You can connect your order with that of the four seasons. And when you unite your good and bad luck with the ghosts and spirits, you can know what the ghosts and spirits know. Would you call that wonderful or not? When you can reach unconditioned empty space, then you become one with the natural order of things.

Two is **unconditioned extinction attained by selection**. Selection means choosing. You might say, "Well, if it's selected, it seems it would be conditioned, wouldn't it?" Yes, the selection is conditioned, but at the time when the extinction is reached, then it is unconditioned. That is why this dharma is not considered to be a conditioned dharma. The first ninety-four dharmas were all conditioned. It is only these six that are Unconditioned Dharmas. When one reaches extinction that is attained by selection, one has no body, and so it belongs to the unconditioned.

Three is **unconditioned extinction that is unselected**. That is when, without making use of the power to choose or select, one's basic nature is purified. The previous dharma, unconditioned extinction attained by selection, is the kind of state of Nirvana certified to by Bodhisattvas of provisional enlightenment. In addition, when those of the Two Vehicles contemplate emptiness by dividing form into its separate characteristics until all marks disappear and form becomes emptied, that it is known as unconditioned extinction attained by selection. Now this dharma, unconditioned extinction that is unselected, refers to the fundamental purification of one's self-nature without the use of any effort of distinction or selection. This is the state certified to by Bodhisattvas of actual enlightenment.

By contrast, Bodhisattvas of provisional enlightenment sever one portion of ignorance in order to certify to one portion of enlightenment. The enlightenment they certify to is directly proportionate to the amount of ignorance they cut off. That is unconditioned extinction attained by selection. However, unconditioned extinction that is unselected is the state certified to by Bodhisattvas of actual enlightenment. This is further subdivided into two categories:

⊞ The Two Divisions of Unconditioned Extinction that is Unselected ⊞

1. Absence of conditioning factors.
2. Fundamental purification of the self-nature.

With the first kind, absence of conditioning factors, the required factors for conditioning are not present. This state of unconditioned extinction that is unselected can sometimes be experienced by ordinary people or those of the Two Vehicles.

Four is **unconditioned unmoving extinction**. Unmoving refers to cultivation of the *samadhi* of not moving. This kind of unmovingness is original and basic stillness. It is not the kind of non-movement attained in the No-Thought Samadhi. Therefore, this is unconditioned unmoving extinction.

Five is **unconditioned extinction of feeling and thinking**. With the previous unconditioned unmoving extinction, one is reborn in the heavens of the Form Realm. With the attainment of unconditioned extinction of feeling and thinking, one is reborn in the Formless Realm. When one reaches the Formless Realm, one's mind is not moved by suffering or by pleasure. There is no concept of what is meant by suffering or what is meant by pleasure. One is not shaken by either of those states.

It is not like we people who, upon encountering a state of suffering cannot stand it; and upon meeting a state of pleasure want to pursue it. We run around in pursuit of things. For example, you hear someone say, "Ah! Here's something that doesn't exist in this country. It's really good to eat!" You say, "Really! I'll try some!" and you go running after flavor. Do you see? That is your mind being moved by pain and pleasure. But when one is certified to this unconditioned extinction of feeling and thinking, pleasure and pain no longer move one's mind. You can experience pleasure and endure pain without any kind of effort on your part. You do not have to use patience to do it. You just basically do not move in the midst of it. This again is fundamentally "Everything's okay." When you are unmoved by suffering or happiness, you have achieved this kind of *samadhi* of unconditioned extinction of feeling and thinking. That is the fifth.

Take a look. When you think, what do you think of? When you feel, what do you feel? You think about and feel pleasure and pain. But when these do not move your mind, then you have achieved unconditioned extinction of feeling and thinking. Are there any of you who cultivate the Way who have managed to cultivate to this state? If you get to this state you can go to the heavens of the Formless Realm, specifically, the Five Heavens of No Return, which are where Arhats of the third fruition abide.

When you have cultivated to the point that you do not register pain or pleasure, then that is like Shariputra's uncle, who held the doctrine of "non-acceptance" of anything. His meaning was that he did not accept pleasure or pain, and this was supposed to indicate that he had that power of *samadhi*. But when the Buddha asked him, "Well, do you accept your own view on this?" Shariputra's uncle was stuck. He could not come up with an answer, because basically his doctrine of non-acceptance was itself a viewpoint. If he was not accepting views, then basically he could not accept his own doctrine. By asking one simple question, the Buddha toppled his doctrine. That is because the uncle still had not reached the state of "Everything's okay." Since Shariputra was still holding this doctrine of non-acceptance, he was thereby defeated. Did he accept his non-acceptance? If he could have been without acceptance or non-acceptance, then there also would have been no victory or defeat. That is the nature of the unconditioned.

Six is **unconditioned True Thusness**. What is True Thusness? You may say, "I've heard this explained before. True Thusness is one's basic Buddhanature, also called Nirvana, and also known as the Nature of the Treasury of the Thus Come One. It has many names. That's True Thusness, isn't it?"

Yes, it is. But you still do not recognize what that is; even less do you know what it is not. What is "that"? It is non-falseness and non-inversion. Being non-false and non-inverted is being "Thus, Thus, Unmoving; clear and constantly understanding." That is True Thusness. In order to know True Thusness, we must first know about the Three Natures.

🄷 The Three Natures 🄷

1. The nature pervasively calculated and attached to.
2. The nature that arises dependent on something else.
3. The perfectly accomplished real nature.

We living beings have the first two kinds of inversion, while True Thusness is the perfectly accomplished real nature.

To illustrate the nature pervasively calculated and attached to, suppose you were walking at night and you thought you had spotted a huge snake on the road ahead. You might shout, "Wow! That's a really long snake! It's several feet long! How horrible!" Seeing a snake in the distance like that is the nature pervasively calculated and attached to, and leads to your being terrified and deciding, "Oh! A snake! I've got to get out of here right away!" So you go running back down the road and overtake a person who had earlier passed the same spot you were approaching when you thought you saw the snake.

The person asks you, "Why are you running?"

You reply, "You just came along that road. Didn't you see the big snake back there?"

"Where?" says the other fellow. "Why don't we go back and see where it is, and we can beat it to death." So the two of you go back, but when you get there it is no longer a snake. It has turned into something else, a piece of rope lying on the road. That it is not a snake is the nature that arises dependent on something else. Considering it to be a snake to begin with was the nature pervasively calculated and attached to. Now it becomes the nature that arises dependent on something else: basically it is a piece of rope. So the nature pervasively calculated and attached to was false, imaginary. However, the nature that arises dependent on something else turns out to be a distortion, for in fact the rope itself is made out of hemp. That it is made of hemp is the perfectly accomplished real nature. What started out as hemp could turn into a piece of rope and then could turn into a snake. Who would you say caused it to transform?

True Thusness is non-false, non-distorted, and not inverted. That is what is meant when it is said of people who have perfected their cultivation that they have ended all falseness and have already exhausted all inversion, so they are no longer upside-down.

That is the perfectly accomplished real nature, also known as True Thusness. However, this True Thusness is still not genuine True Thusness. Because, what you can detect can still not be called real. Real True Thusness is that basically there is no True Thusness. Real True Thusness is nothing at all. There is no common identity and no distinction. There are no dharmas and no non-dharmas. This refers to the basic substance of each and every dharma, in the same way that water has waves, but the waves are not the water. Water is its own substance. And True Thusness is the basic substance of all dharmas. If it were not for True Thusness, then dharmas would lack a basic substance. It is like the rope. The rope's basic substance is hemp. True Thusness is not singular, and yet it is non-dual. It is identical and yet not different; not dharmas and yet not non-dharmas. That is genuine True Thusness, the sixth unconditioned dharma.

Shastra

What is meant by there being no self?
There are, in general, two kinds of
Non-self: one, the Non-self of Pudgala,
and two, the Non-self of Dharmas.

Commentary

What is meant by there being no self? Someone says, "What do you mean 'no self'? I'm right here. I'm truly and actually here, so how can you say I don't exist? Aren't you just trying to cheat us?" That way of thinking is just a case of misunderstanding dharmas. If you did understand the hundred dharmas, then you would know that it is impossible for there to be a self.

There are, in general, two kinds of Non-self: one, the Non-self of Pudgala.

⊞ The Two kinds of Non-Self ⊞

1. The non-self of *pudgala*. (no me or mine)
2. The non-self of dharmas. (no *svabhava*—inherent nature)

Pudgala is a Sanskrit word which translates as "multiple grasping at destinies." This refers to numerous comings and goings, revolving in the Six Destinies.

⊞ The Six Destinies Three Good Paths ⊞

1. gods
2. *asuras*
3. people

⊞ Three Evil Paths ⊞

4. animals
5. ghosts
6. hell-beings

All ordinary people and all creatures just keep turning around and around on the revolving wheel of the six paths, which are also known as the Six Ordinary Dharma Realms.

⊞ The Four Sagely Paths ⊞

1. Buddhas
2. Bodhisattvas
3. Those Enlightened to Conditions
4. Sound Hearers

Altogether those make the Ten Dharma Realms. Where do these ten come from? They are all just the manifestation of a single thought of yours or mine. If your mind thinks of cultivating and becoming a Buddha, then in the future you will be able to become a Buddha. Your thinking of doing that makes it happen. If you think about cultivation to become a Bodhisattva, in the future you will to become a Bodhisattva. If your mind thinks about becoming a person of the Two Vehicles—a Sound Hearer or One Enlightened to Conditions—then you will become one or the other. If your mind thinks about ascending to the heavens, in the future you can be born in the heavens.

All you need do is hold the five precepts and practice the ten good acts and you will gain rebirth in the heavens. If you say, "Well, I want to be a person," then just offer up all good conduct and do not do any evil and you can be a person. If you are thinking of becoming an *asura*, then get angry all the time and think about killing people. If you do that, then that in itself is the Dharma Realm of the *asuras* and in the future you will become an *asura*. Those are the three good paths.

Then there are the three evil paths. If you are constantly, tremendously greedy all the time, then you can fall into the hells. If your hatred is heavy, if you keep getting angry from morning to night, you can turn into a hungry ghost. If you are extremely stupid, then you will end up as an animal. So if you have greed, anger, and foolishness you will fall into the evil paths. If you cultivate precepts, *samadhi* and wisdom, then you will be born into the three good paths and will have the possibility of becoming a Buddha in the future. Turning in the Six Paths is dangerous business. There is an old saying about it:

> Out of the horse's belly, into the womb of a cow.
> How many times have we gone in and out of Yama's halls?
> First one swings by Shakra's Palace,
> Then plunges down into Lord Yama's pot.

One just finishes being a horse and ends up back in the womb of a cow. How many times have you done that? Too many. You are so familiar with that route by Yama's door that you could walk it with your eyes closed. You do not know how many times you have done it. You may make it up to the Jade Emperor's heavenly halls for a time, but once again you fall into the pot of boiling oil that King Yama always keeps hot. Becoming a person is made from the mind. Becoming an animal also comes about from the mind. If you act like an animal, in the future you will become an animal. If you act like a person, in the future you will be a person. If you act like a ghost, in the future you will be a ghost.

Some people say they do not believe in ghosts. Why do they say that? It is because they themselves are ghosts, and they are afraid others will recognize them as such. So they are always telling others not to believe there are such things as ghosts. I often say that basically there is no real difference between Buddhas and ghosts. If you are evil to the ultimate point, then you are a ghost. If you are good to the ultimate point, then you are a Buddha. If you cultivate to the point of becoming enlightened, then you are a Buddha. If you do not get enlightened and keep being stupid, then you are a ghost. Basically there is no difference.

Some people believe in the Buddha and say, "Buddhas exist," but they do not believe that there are ghosts. They say, "There aren't any ghosts." Why do they say that? "I haven't seen any ghosts," they argue, "so I don't believe any such things exist."

I ask them, "Well have you seen Buddhas?" I can safely ask them that, because if they have not seen ghosts, then they have not seen Buddhas. So I say to them, "You have never seen Buddhas either, so why do you believe in them? If you haven't seen them, you shouldn't believe in them either, right?

They say, "I have seen Buddha images." Well there are pictures of ghosts around, too. If you see Buddha images and therefore believe in Buddhas, then when you see pictures of ghosts, shouldn't you believe in ghosts? I will tell you right now that those who do not believe in ghosts are this way because they do not have the wisdom to believe ghosts exist. They do not have the true and actual, perfectly interpenetrating and unobstructed wisdom to know this principle.

If you do not believe in ghosts, you should not believe in the Buddhas, either. There just would not be anything at all. How would that be? Of course, it is true that originally there is nothing at all. Basically there is no self nor people, nor Buddhas, nor ghosts—nothing at all. But you have to reach that state. You must truly have achieved the level of no self. It cannot be that you say there is no self, but when time comes to eat you eat more than anyone else. There is a self in that. Or when it comes time to work you say, "I heard the Dharma Master say to be without self, so I shouldn't do any work." But when the time comes to eat, your self is suddenly in existence again, because you definitely have to eat. You must genuinely without self. That means being without any attachments. If you are attached to the existence of a self, then you have an attachment to self, presenting causes and conditions that obstruct the Way. Hence you should have no self.

Even if you are without a self, you still need to be without dharmas. Dharmas must also disappear. Dharmas exist for the sake of the self, so if there is no self, what do you need dharmas for? Then dharmas have no use, either. If you do not have a self, then you have broken your attachment to self, which is also the obstacle of afflictions. If you get rid of dharmas, then you have broken through the attachment to dharmas, as well as through the obstacle of the known.

⊞ The Two Obstacles ⊞

1. The obstacle of afflictions.
2. The obstacle of the known.

The obstacle of the known manifests when you have not broken through your attachment to dharmas. You say things such as, "Take a look at me! See? I understand all six hundred rolls of the *prajna sutras.* I've read them I don't know how many times. I can lecture the *Dharma Flower Sutra* and explain the *Shurangama Sutra.*" This indicates that you have the obstacle of the known. Whatever it is, you know about it. In this way you produce an obstacle, the obstacle being, "I know and you do not know. I can lecture and you cannot lecture. I can cultivate and you cannot cultivate. I have all kinds of Way virtue, and you don't have any Way virtue. I have wisdom, and you don't have wisdom."

If dharmas were also empty, then you would not have this obstacle, but would certify to the second kind of non-self, which is **the non-self of dharmas.**

Then, although you understand dharmas, it would be just as if you did not. "What in the world is the use of studying Dharma, anyway, then?" you may conclude. Well, if you can know and yet not know, then that would really be knowing. That would be having real wisdom. Then you would have broken through the obstacle of the known and the obstacle of afflictions.

Why do you have afflictions? They come from your attachment to self. If you did not have a self, where would you go to find afflictions? Therefore, the non-self of *pudgala* smashes the obstacle of afflictions. Second is the obstacle of the known. The non-self of dharmas smashes the obstacle of the known, so this passage discusses the non-self of *pudgala* and the non-self of dharmas to explain the last part of the Buddha's quote that began the Shastra:

> As the World Honored One has said, all dharmas have
> no self.

So it cannot be that you simply break through the attachment to self and yet harbor an attachment to how well you comprehend dharmas. You also have to renounce the thought of understanding dharmas. This absence of self refers to one's view of self, not to the physical body. One should be devoid of a view of self and a view of dharmas.

All ordinary people are attached to the existence of a self. Those who manage not to be attached to a self become attached to dharmas. The Buddha knew what was in the minds of living beings, and he wanted to break through their obstacles of afflictions and their obstacles of the known. He spoke all kinds of Dharma for the purpose of destroying those obstacles. However, it is really easy to talk about having no view of self, but when a person gets to the point of not having a self, he thinks, "Hey! Look at me! I don't have a self!" So who is talking about not having a self? Who is that? Or else he speaks the Dharma coming and going and says, "I speak Dharma better than anybody! But it's not me speaking, it's the Bodhisattvas speaking," in a roundabout way ascribing to himself a Bodhisattva position. Then, sitting upon that Bodhisattva pedestal he has fashioned for himself, he still has a self. So you see, it is not easy. It is not something that can be brought about merely by making that claim. You cannot just say, "I have no self" for it to be the case. Your "no self" still harbors a self within it. So in discussing dharmas you need to understand them in a fundamental way. It cannot be that you seem to understand them but really do not. Anyone with any knowledge will catch on to that very quickly and know that you are simply a person who is fond of wearing high hats. Your view of self is still not empty.

Now let us investigate the self. The head is called a "head." The hair is called "hair." The eyes are called "eyes." The ears are called "ears." The nose is called a "nose." And it goes on like that down through the hands being called "hands," and the feet being called "feet," and the fingernails being called "fingernails," and on down to the eighty-four thousand pores being called "pores." The three hundred and sixty bones are called "bones," and yet each has its own individual name. But if you search throughout your entire body, from the top of your head to the soles of your feet, where can you find a "self"? What location can be given the name "self"? What bit of flesh has that name? What drop of blood is known as the "self"? Keep searching for the location of that "self," and you will find that in the entire body there is not a single place that can be called "self". So why are you still attached to a "self"?

You say, "I know where I am." It is fine if you really know. However, it may be that you do not truly, purely know, and that what you know is a kind of defiled dharma. But do you recognize your true, actual, pure self: your basic self-nature? Do you ultimately know where that is? Well, look for it. See if you can find it.

I am here lecturing and I have a self. You are there listening with "selves." So you wonder, "If I don't come and listen to the Sutras, does that mean I have no self?" No. If you do not come and listen to the Sutras, it just means your "self" is not here listening to the Sutras; but it does not mean that your self does not exist. However, if you could be here listening to the Sutras as if you were not here, then you would have attained a little bit of skill.

"Right!" someone thinks. "I have really got that kind of skill, because just now I had the false thought about going to a bar to drink some wine and about how fine that wine would taste."

That is just running off; it is not really being gone. It was just indulging in an idle thought. Many people here are having idle thoughts, and their "selves" are running off. But that does not mean their "selves" are gone. If you have a self, then it can run off. It should be that there is "no going and no coming."

You neither run off, nor do you stay. If you are that way, then that is pretty much "it". Ultimately what's "it"? It is non-self.

Now I have finished lecturing the Shastra, and you can just consider it as if I had not said a thing, because there should be no self. I did not lecture and you did not listen. Everyone is devoid of self. This non-self is wonderful; it is the true non-self.

Glossary

Buddha nature The potential to be fully awakened and wise, which is inherent in all beings. The Buddha nature is non-dual and all beings are endowed with it. It does not increase in an enlightened being, nor is it less in a confused being.

Complete Precepts The precepts received at full ordination in both the Mahayana and Therevada traditions. These precepts were set forth by Shakaymuni Buddha during the course of his teaching of disciples. There are 250 Bhikshu (Buddhist monk) precepts and 348 Bhikshuni (Buddhist nun) precepts.

Confucius Born in 551 B.C., he became a great educator and sage, who throughout his life tirelessly propagated the virtues of humaneness and righteousness and the doctrines of filiality, fraternal respect, loyalty, and trustworthiness.

Dharma doors Method of practice. There are said to be eighty-four thousand of them.

Guest dust A term for afflictions, which are transient like a guest and defiling like dust.

Five Schools of Buddhism
1. Teaching School: the study of the texts and doctrines of Buddhism;
2. Vinaya School: the deportment and rules; the precepts of Buddhism.
3. Chan School: meditation based on proper knowledge and proper views.

4. Pure Land School: the recitation of Amitabha Buddha's name and related study and practice.
5. The Secret School: practice involving mantras and mudras.

Form Realm & Formless Realm These, along with the desire realm make up the Triple Realm. Beings in the Triple Realm are subject to birth and death.

Jade Emperor A deity revered within Daoism and popular Chinese religion. Also equated with the God of Christianity, and with Shakra—Indra—within the Hindu pantheon. He is lord of the second heaven of the desire realm.

Kalpa A long span of time.

King Yama. King of death There are ten Yamas who sit in judgment after death.

Mencius Lived in the 3rd-4th centuries B. C. and carried on the orthodox Confucian tradition, propagating the Way.

Middle Way The Buddhist concept of avoiding extremes by balancing oneself in the midst of dualities.

Nature of the Treasury of the Thus Come One Our inherent pure and enlightened nature.

Nirvana A state of ultimate tranquility, perfect quiescence realized by enlightened sages.

Precepts Rules governing moral behavior set forth by the Buddha. The five for lay people are: no killing, no stealing, no sexual misconduct, no lying, and no intoxicants.

Self-nature See Buddha nature.

Shakra See Jade Emperor.

Ten Good Acts Refraining from greed, hatred, and stupidity in the mind; from harsh speech, back-biting, loose speech, and false speech with the mouth; and killing, stealing, and lust with the body.

Twelve Links of Conditioned Co-Production They are:
1. ignorance, which generates
2. activity, which generates
3. consciousness, which generates
4. name and form, which generate
5. the six sense organs, which generate
6. contact, which generates
7. feeling, which generates

8. craving, which generates
9. grasping, which generates
10. becoming, which generates
11. birth, which generates
12. old age and death. The reversing of this sequence brings about the ending of these conditions.

Vimalakirti An enlightened layman.

Way-virtue Refers to doing virtuous deeds as one practices the Way.

White Yang Buddha Refers to Maitreya, the next Buddha.Index

Index

C

D

M

N

P

U

Directory

The City of Ten Thousand Buddhas
4951 Bodhi Way,
Ukiah, CA 95482
T: 707-462-0939
F: 707-462-0949
www.drba.org

Buddhist Text Translation Society
4951 Bodhi Way,
Ukiah, CA 95482
www.bttsonline.org

The City of Dharma Realm
1029 West Capitol Ave.,
West Sacramento, CA 95691
T: 916-374-8268
F: 916-374-8234

The International Translation Institute
1777 Murchison Drive,
Burlingame, CA 94010
T: 650-692-5912
F: 650-692-5056

Gold Mountain Monastery
800 Sacramento Street
San Francisco, CA 94108
T: 415-421-6117
F: 415-788-6001

Gold Sage Monastery
11455 Clayton Road,
San Jose, CA 95127
T: 408-923-7243
F: 408-923-1064

Gold Wheel Monastery
235 N. Avenue 58,
Los Angeles, CA 90042
T: 323-258-6668
F: 323-258-3619

Long Beach Monastery
3361 East Ocean Boulevard,
Long Beach, CA 90803
T/F: 310-438-8902

Gold Buddha Monastery
248 E 11th Avenue,
Vancouver, B.C.,
V5T 2C3, Canada
T: 604-709-0248
F: 604-684-3754

Gold Summit Monastery
233 1st Avenue West,
Seattle, WA 98119
T: 206-284-6690
F: 206-284-6918

Avatamsaka Vihara
9601 Seven Locks Road,
Bethesda, MD 20817-9997
T/F: 301-469-8300

Avatamsaka Monastery
1009 4th Avenue, S.W.
Calgary AB, T2P 0K8,
Canada
T/F: 403-234-0644

Gold Dharma Monastery
3645 Florida Avenue
Kenner, LA 70065
T: 504-466-1626

Dharma Realm Buddhist Books Dist. Society
85 Chung-hsiao E. Road,
Sec. 6, Fl. 11
Taipei, Taiwan
T: 02-2786-3022
F: 02-2786-2674

Amitabha Monastery
7, Su-chien-hui,
Chih-nan Village, Shou-feng,
Hualien County, Taiwan
T: 03-865-1956
F: 03-865-3426

Dharma Realm Sagely Monastery
20, Tong-hsi Shan-chuang,
Hsing-lung Village Liu-kuei,
Kaohsiung County, Taiwan
T: 07-689-3713
F: 07-689-3870

Prajna Guanyin Sagely Monastery
Batu 51/2, Jalan Sungai Besi,
Salak Selatan, 57100,
Kuala Lumpur, Malaysia
T: 03-7982-6560
F: 03-7980-1272

Dharma Realm Guanyin Sagely Monastery
161, Jalan Ampang, 50450,
Kuala Lumpur, Malaysia
T: 03-2164-8055
F: 03-2163-7118

Malaysia Dharma Realm Buddhist
Asso. Penang Branch 32-32C,
Jalan Tan Sri Teh Ewe Lim,
11600 Jelutong, Penang,
Malaysia
T: 04-281-7728
F: 04-281-7798

Lotus Vihara Monastery
136 Jalan Sekolah,
45600 Batang Berjuntai,
Selangor, Malaysia
T: 03-3271-9439

Fa Yuan Sagely
1, Jalan Utama,
Taman Serdang Raya,
43300, Seri Kembangan,
Selangor, Malaysia
T: 03-8948-5688